IT'S *not* ABOUT THE MONEY

3 Steps to Become a Wealthy Woman

catherine morgan

authors
AND CO.

CONTENTS

DEDICATION

I dedicate this book to G & T. Not a refreshing drink, but my two boys George and Thomas, who make me smile every single day. Also to my husband Gareth who without a shadow of a doubt has shown me what love is ... and to sweet little dog Rosie who keeps me company whilst creating tidal waves of change from my home office.

FOREWORD

When Catherine asked me to write the foreword for this book, her request couldn't have come at a better time.

I was just reading a different book on money for women and was left wanting more. Yes that book was inspiring - but inspiring isn't enough. I needed a book that not only inspired you to take action but actually walked you through practical tools and techniques to apply to life, a step-by-step approach.

THIS BOOK IS THAT BOOK. It's a game changer!

I first met Catherine online. She invited me to be a guest on her podcast and I'll be honest - my instinct was 'Woah - she's so brave talking about money like that!' - a reaction I've learned through this book was based on my own money story and the perceptions and meaning that I attached to money.

Now that I know her and would call her a friend, I'd say she IS brave. And you should be too!

Back in 2017, after 30 years in TV and radio that saw me fronting Blue Peter, Live & Kicking, Top of the Pops - I was fronting the Breakfast Show for Heart, living in a lovely home in Oxfordshire with my husband and two children and, on the surface, had it all. But I realised - I was living the life that had presented itself to me. I wasn't LIVING LIFE - life was LIVING ME. I was living a reactive, not proactive, reality. I knew there was more for me in life, but I just didn't know how to access it.

So - I did something about it. I hit RESET. I took control. I threw myself into studying NLP and qualifying as a self-development coach and I can honestly say, I felt alive inside ... I was finally living my purpose. I know that you are likely reading this book because you want to live your life on purpose too.

I'm passionate that we all need to be playing all-out and living the life we were born to live.

In my coaching, money is actually one of my 9 key areas of life we need to pay attention to in order to feel fulfilled and getting vulnerable and honest around our own money stories is part of that.

The first step towards you being brave is buying this book.

The second step is reading it.

The third is implementing it!

I implore you not to let this be just another book on the bedside table stack. It has the power to change your life! It's full of tangible tools and techniques you can apply to your life right now to bring about powerful change and set you on the path to living the life you were born to live!

Step up! Be BRAVE!

Katy Hill

INTRODUCTION

 'The way we treat money is a mirror reflection of how we treat ourselves.'

— **CATHERINE MORGAN**

*Our ability **to receive wealth** is mirrored in our ability to **be loved and feel loved**.*

Picture a 13-year-old girl back in May, 1994. It is lunchtime and she returns to her classroom to fetch her jacket just as dark clouds begin to gather outside. On her way out, she notices something on the wall. Somebody has written on her piece of work that was pinned to the board. Moving closer she notices two words marked in thick black marker pen - *Dog Breath*. She panics - scrubbing at the words before anybody else might see them - but they're permanent, indelible. Running out of the classroom to the refuge of the bathroom she is confronted by Katy, who she knows is the culprit. The bully. Katy pushes her out into the playground where a group of older girls waits. They form a circle with this girl inside and the ringleader pushes her across to the other side. The others push her back ... side to side ... side to side she is pushed. They rip open her school bag, her sandwiches falling to the ground. The ringleader picks up her bottle of squash and pours it over the girl's head, the sweet odour consuming her thick, long, brown hair. 'Dog Breath!' they chant, over and over, until the rattling old school bell rings.

She is saved.

That afternoon the girl runs home, avoiding the school bus journey she normally takes. She does not tell a soul. It becomes her secret – the first of many. She is not worthy, she is not good enough. She continues to hide away, but it isn't enough to just hide. This girl stops eating because, maybe, that would help the toothpaste she uses every morning to hide that dog breath. She hides her food and for years food is the enemy, the *bully* ... a way for her to hide her shame. She begins to keep a diary of everything she eats and how many calories she consumes - usually 100-500 a day. She smuggles her dinner upstairs, pretending she is studying, and flushes it down the toilet. Or she stores it in a carrier bag before taking it out to the bin late at night. She does sit-ups in bed until her body cries with pain. Secretly, she is screaming for someone to notice that she isn't eating, just so that they'd ask if she is OK.

Over time, money is used to buy more clothes to hide this girl's shame. It consumes her life. She will not wear a pair of jeans for longer than a few hours as she believes that every time she sits down in them they'll crease and make her look fat. She becomes obsessed with anything to do with anorexia and bulimia and keeps a book of magazine clippings as inspiration. It takes around two hours every day to go through ten outfit changes, so angry and anxious is she about how she looks. She learns quite early on that ice-cream is easier to throw up. Some days she is so starved of food that her body screams out for carbs, so she raids the cupboards and then throws it all back up again. And yet, no matter how much or how meticulously she controls the food that she puts into her body, she never feels good enough. She is never slim enough or pretty enough. This girl wants to look perfect.

It's not about the money.

At the age of 22 this girl becomes a financial adviser, helping others with their money. She secretly overspends every single month and this cycle of control and bad habits continues for at least a decade. At the bank she is helping people to manage money whilst feeling increasingly worse about her own. The shame is too much. *'I am a financial adviser, I should know what to do.'*

Living in debt becomes comfortable. She blows and blows her budget down ... £10,000, £20,000, £30,000 ... until one day after ten years, as she sits on her little red couch in Jersey, surrounded by clothes she's been hoarding for years, she realises that it is time to let go of the shame, time to let go of the bully. Time to stop comparing herself to everybody else. Money is never going to bring the happiness she desperately seeks because it was *never about the money*. She just wants to be loved, to *feel* loved. To love herself.

With hard, transformational work and a willingness to change, this girl eventually lets go of the bully, marries the love of her life, has her first child and sets up her first small business. Over time and with increasing confidence her relationship with both her money and her body changes. And then, in 2013, she experiences another major life event that sees her second child fighting for his life.

On 1st October 2013, Thomas is just five weeks old. This morning, he doesn't want to feed, he doesn't want to be held, he doesn't want to be cuddled, doesn't want to be touched. As he sleeps, he makes strange grunting noises. When lifted out of his Moses basket he lays still, looking up at the ceiling with an expression on his face as if each blink is agony. His hands and feet are like ice. Then he begins to scream.

They are seen by a doctor within minutes of arriving at A&E. Thomas's skin has begun to mottle and they're raced to resuscitation. A dozen medical staff surround him and his mother in a surreal, calm environment. One doctor keeps using the word *sepsis* but it means very little to this girl. A day or so later they are told that Thomas had bacterial meningitis.

This girl hadn't known that sepsis was the biggest killer of newborn babies. She hadn't known that signs of sepsis are cold hands and feet, and grunting during sleep. So when they come out of hospital she feels proud of moving so quickly and saving his life ... but this is pride with a flip side. What if she hadn't? What if not knowing those things about sepsis had resulted in not acting as quickly as she did? A period of post-traumatic stress disorder follows and she becomes obsessive with Thomas' routine and her need to control it. And, along with needing to control Thomas' routine, the urge to control other things comes back with a vengeance and her spending once again spirals out of control.

And so begins yet another cycle of spending in an attempt to feel better. This girl, once again, has little or no insight into her finances and no control over her money, but the PTSD diagnosis kick-starts a journey of recovery.

The difference, this time, is that this girl knows she can change. She has solid evidence of doing just that, and she knows *how* to do it. It takes time - she has to be honest with herself and identify the thought processes that have led her down this path again - and using the tools she developed during that previous period of transformation, this girl regains control over those thoughts and, as a result, her behaviours.

With her head clear enough to see how trauma had triggered her overspending, she is finally able to look at her spending habits and put two actions in place. Her biggest area of overspend is with *Amazon*, so she begins leaving her purchases in the online shopping basket for 48 hours. If, after that time, she feels she REALLY needs those items, she gives herself permission to click through to checkout. She also diverts all the marketing emails she receives into a different online folder in order to avoid spontaneous spending. It is during this time that she has a lightbulb moment: spending is actually EMOTIONAL, not rational. In order to change her habits this girl has to find the root cause and acknowledge the deeper relationship she has with money. She has to navigate her own *money mindset*. She has to let go of trying to control money. Money isn't something to be controlled.

It's not about the money.

In letting go of that control, this girl asks herself a series of questions: What did I have a lot of growing up? What do I want more of in my life right now? What would having more of this mean to me? What do I want less of? What would I need to be saying to myself or doing to make it happen? Who do I need to forgive in order to feel free with money? And in so doing, she realises that what we spend is what we value. What we save is what we seek. What we give is what we long for. What we yearn for is who we want to be - our being ... our *wellbeing*. Financial wellbeing is learning to discover who we are and what we are longing for.

Our stories reveal so many patterns and hidden meanings about our lives. Our stories reveal the things that matter the most. Do you have your own story? Do you have a money secret that has hurt you, that affects how you behave with money today?

It's not about the money.

Problems with money are not solved with the exclusive knowledge of knowing how to manage it. We can know everything there is to know about money but not follow the advice. Our money behaviours and stories become judgement, guilt, fear of not having enough, looking stupid, being exposed, being bullied. When we feel these emotions around money, when we feel shame, we're saying 'I am ashamed', 'I don't have enough', 'I spend too much', 'I don't want to look stupid', 'I don't want to be exposed', 'if I can avoid talking about money, maybe I can avoid the shame around money'. But feeling that emotion isn't bad. It shows us it matters, *we* matter. And ignoring these emotions can damage us. They consume our thoughts and energy, they take our sleep and they threaten healthy relationships.

We cannot change our secrets but we can change the meaning we attach to them. These feelings are not who we are and they're not who money is.

It's not about the money.

Debt can be comfortable. It may be for you. Your wealth creation level may be just within your comfort zone, but that doesn't necessarily make you bad with money. Taking necessary risks doesn't make you bad. Debt can sometimes protect us - from the bully, from acknowledging deep-rooted secrets and traumas.

People think traumas are the BIG traumas – abuse, loss of a loved one, being attacked, war. But actually trauma is simply any disruption to the nervous system. It is any **event that exceeds our capacity to cope and instead causes a disruption in the way we function emotionally**. Such events aren't inherently life-threatening, but rather *ego-threatening*, as they cause people to feel helpless in their circumstances.

At the age of 24 this girl is confronted again by the bully, but this time, with a heart full of self-worth, the adult version of this girl whispers to herself: 'You are enough' - and with that, the secret has gone. She is heard. She is seen. She matters.

You matter. *You* are seen. *You* are heard. *You* are enough.

Money challenges are not really about the money but the meaning and the power that we give to it. This is often a mirror reflection of what is going on in our life or has gone on in our childhood ... how we feel about ourselves. I want to share my story as a reminder that no matter how tough things are, or how impossible it may seem, you can thrive financially. You can step into those shoes and feel comfortable (and look gorgeous at the same time!) And you'll look back and think: 'I am good enough. I always have been and I always will.'

It's not about the money.

The way we feel about money is actually a reflection of the way we feel about ourselves.

Just read that again: *the way we feel about money is actually a reflection of the way we feel about ourselves.*

Are you focusing on the wrong thing?

Imagine this scenario: Sarah wants more money because she wants to go on more holidays, travel the world with her family and pay off the credit card that she's been using at times she feels low, bored, stressed, lacking in self-confidence. Sarah makes more money and is delighted because she can now pay off that credit card and book the holiday she saw her friend go on last summer. Within three months, Sarah has added another £3,000 onto her credit card and the money has all gone.

By focusing on *more* money, we are focusing on *the* money. And if the underlying belief is that we don't deserve money, we won't keep hold of it. In fact we will likely start noticing things that need paying for - the washing machine breaks down, the car tyres burst. The energy that we have around receiving the extra money we wanted is not positive energy. It is rooted in negative experiences - shame, guilt, judgement, regret.

A year after my five-week-old son almost died of sepsis, I decided that my relationship with money, and myself, needed to change. I sat in my office at the bank thinking 'I wonder how many people feel like I did the day that I was in hospital with Thomas? How many people have felt the guilt and shame I felt because of the jargon used with me in there? How many feel the same because of the jargon used in financial services?' I didn't know what sepsis was. I didn't know that the obvious signs were cold hands and cold feet, grunting in their sleep and not feeding. I felt a deep sense of shame. 'I am a bad mother,' I said to myself. 'I should have known this.' My clients say the same when talking about money: 'I am bad with money.' 'I should know this.' We attach our sense of being, our sense of self, to money. But money is not *who* we are.

In psychology, our sense of self is defined as *'the way a person thinks about and views his or her traits, beliefs, and purpose within the world.'* From the moment we are born, we are exposed to information that can teach us about who we are. We use self-referential language such as *I* to reflect to the world who we are, but these are often statements that don't belong to us. They are statements that we have been given.

Emily was five when she first heard from her mother: 'You are useless with money.' She had dropped her purse down the drain at a fairground. Amelia was four when she tried to pick up a penny from the floor and her father told her 'You are so dirty. That coin is filthy and doesn't belong to you.'

The words *you are* define our perceptions of our identity. We have been programmed with limitations that hold us back from feeling worthy of wealth. We create emotion around each of these experiences and thoughts and these emotions guide our behaviours. We need to separate money from our sense of self. Just imagine that for a moment. How different would you feel if the emotions around money were no longer limiting you?

Why is money so emotional?

 'We cannot solve our problems with the same thinking we used when we created them.

— **ALBERT EINSTEIN**

Just like thoughts, emotions have frequencies. Emotions are energy in motion. Emotion affects our mood, attitude and personality. When we make money decisions based on our emotions, we create an emotional connection. When we personalise the wealth that we witness around us, we expand our emotional wealth. Let's say that you witness wealth around you in a neighbour or someone you follow online. Your response to that is based on your emotional perception. But in reality, even that person who holds more wealth than you has concerns about losing it. We are all trapped, somehow, in a feeling of emotional poverty.

Money is also emotional because of the meaning or the perception that we attach to it. We've all experienced situations involving money, whether it's walking in the supermarket with Mum or witnessing arguments about money at home. The experiences we had as children prior to the age of six become the belief system by which we operate today, but the emotion is not so much in the experience itself as the perception we give to that event. Perceptions are acquired. Some of them are right and some of them are wrong, hence why two people can experience the same horrific turbulence on a flight and create two entirely different perceptions of that journey. The younger version of us records all the instances of negativity, because they are *life or death* moments when the *fight or flight* response of the brain wants to keep that child safe. Such memories leave an imprint on the brain, which files them away like a book in a library for later events so that the brain can keep us safe by reminding us about the beliefs. A single moment of powerlessness will be perceived by the brain as a threat to its survival.

As adults, we look for further proof of these negative experiences in order to feel safe. In truth, we can't change our memories around money but we can change the perceptions we attach to them. We call this *reframing* and we will explore this later in this book. Reframing helps create cognitive shifts to change the perception, the meaning we've attached to a particular event.

Think about a memory you have around money. What did you hear? What did you see? Feel? What belief do you think that gave you about money? Money was greedy? Evil, shameful, caused arguments, scarce, abundant, trapping, used as power over someone, hard to come by, easy to make, hard to keep hold of, fun, secret? Our body stores these memories as energy. We feel a physical reaction to them - sadness, fear, greed, shame - often in the stomach, chest, throat, heart. All these beliefs control our biology - our lives are run by our unconscious minds and every single experience we have prior to the age of six creates these beliefs. Up until this age we were just observing and downloading the information around us. We are in 100% unconscious mode. Our consciousness doesn't even start to develop until the age of six so prior to that we are in this super learning state. This is why young children can learn multiple languages with ease. Every single event creates a memory and these all group together to create our sense of self. In effect, our relationship with money is one of the most important and longest relationships we have.

In order to feel good, be good and do good, we must work *with* our emotions, feel safe to express them, let them flow ... otherwise we will store them, risking an impact on our physical and mental wellbeing. The trauma of money memories can create physical illness, anxiety, fear, shame, guilt. Learning to live in the here and now without shame, blame or guilt around money can unlock opportunities and growth. It can help us to feel connected in our relationships and inside our communities. It enables and motivates us to work towards a future that will nurture us. Financial education is only part of this journey. Education alone will not prevent us from self-sabotaging. It will not prevent us from overspending or underearning. It will not help with sticking to a financial plan or breaking through our own boundaries when we overgive our time. These behaviours are driven by our need for human connection and ultimately to feel loved and safe. The key is to be able to hold onto the emotions that support wealth: joy, happiness, gratitude, love.

Having an understanding of how we communicate with ourselves and each other at an unconscious level enables us to shift from our current state. If we operate from a state of *not enoughness*, it doesn't matter how much money we earn or make, we may not feel deserving to keep it or we may feel comfortable keeping it but not comfortable spending it. Hoarding cash is all well and good, but it prevents us from growing our money for a secure lifetime.

If you are a woman reading this book you will know that we make choices and sacrifices in our lives that wreak havoc with our finances. The focus on money changes as we grow through different life cycles. First, there is the growing up cycle - going through full-time education, possibly university. Our money challenges during that cycle are very different from those we have in pre-retirement, and there are times we may have to utilize *good* - not bad - debt. We're not taught how to manage money so we come out of university and into a career - the second life cycle - when it's all about equipping ourselves for the life ahead. The next stage is going into a relationship and thinking about building a family. Building a family has its own financial challenges and as women we may need time out of the workplace, putting pressure on the household income and reducing our pension contributions, resulting in a big savings or investing gap. The final two cycles are around caring and the end of life. Our parents begin to age and it's often women looking after them, leading to more financial and emotional pressure. Even with our Superwoman pants on it's important to recognize if we're in one of those challenging life cycles. Who can we ask for support?

Most women outlive their male partners and 65% will be either single or divorced by the time they reach their 80s or 90s, creating a huge and growing wealth gap. What would happen if women had more power? More wealth? How many of us are making decisions around money in our households right now? How many of us are investing? If more women invested, the economy would grow faster - fact. When women invest, we stick to our decisions more often than men. We are less likely to make rash investment decisions. We're more cautious in our approach. Ironically, the reason we're not investing is that we're not confident to do so. It is changing, though. Whilst wealthy men have historically made all the decisions, we are seeing more and more women holding financial power, setting up their own businesses, advising others.

It's a conundrum. Money is often perceived to be overwhelming, stressful and complicated and yet our natural mind is happy for us to bury our heads in the sand and continue the habits that keep us stuck. We believe that having *more* money will make all of that overwhelm, stress and complication go away. And sure enough, having money creates freedom and opportunity ... but it won't necessarily make those problems disappear or reduce the emotions keeping us stuck and limiting our potential.

In truth, money costs us twice - once with its financial, concrete price and then with the emotional toll it takes. Strange that, because money in itself is just an object - a coin, a note, a bank balance. There is no emotion in that coin, note or number on your screen, and yet it inspires so much - guilt, shame, judgement, not enoughness, fear, anxiety, happiness, pleasure, gratitude.

But **it's not about the money.**

We give so much of our power away to the feelings inspired by money and our relationship with it. It's time to redirect that power, to move from feeling *dis*empowered to *emp*owered ... from not good enough to more than good enough ... from unworthy to deserving.

We need to look at money through a *trauma-informed* lens. We need to distil the little traumas and the big traumas from our unconscious mind, from our belief systems, in order to change our perception of money from disempowerment to one of empowerment.

This book will help you to do that.

Because you are enough.

You are already a wealthy woman.

Catherine x

It's not about the money - *How to deserve, create and grow more money*

Step 1 - Past (Deserve)

Welcome to the beginning ... the first step on one of the most important journeys you will ever make. And this first step is the most crucial. Why? Because you can have no power over your future unless you know where you've come from.

Just as Dickens' Scrooge changed his life by being forced to revisit his past, examine his present and get a glimpse of his future - a painful journey that transformed his fortunes and gave him a second chance at a life he would be proud of - you can do the same with your financial path. In this first step you will look at how you got here - your *financial past*. You will consider the meaning and perception you give to money and see how, if you were empowered and more confident around money, you'd change the world. Here's the thing - the detail is not in the *amount* of money you think you need, but your relationship with it.

Most decisions you make come from a place of emotion, triggered by a core belief. This is why money is a source of stress - not managing it well, not having enough, can lead you to feel personally liable. It attacks your sense of wellbeing and your sense of self. Your brain goes into *fight, flight or freeze* mode when triggered - by trauma, your past, your parents - and it all relates to your financial past, the decisions you've made around money, the thought patterns, the beliefs, the things you were told about it - *money doesn't grow on trees, you have to work hard to make money, everything has to be perfect* - as well as the things you weren't told.

In this step you will uncover your own money story. You will learn how you communicate love, security, freedom, hope, opportunity and power through money, all whilst not even wishing to talk about it. You will learn how, whilst money is a taboo subject (or so the story goes) *not* talking about it fuels the 'story' - with shame, guilt and responsibility.

Being clear on your internal story, your *money narrative,* will provide clarity for your pathway to financial security and wellbeing. From this step - and this is the *emotional* step - you'll learn how to deal with the self-sabotaging emotions you have around money. It is one of, if not THE most important step in learning how to deserve more money. Money is both a powerful enabler *and* disabler. Which of these jobs are you giving it right now?

Step 2 - Present (Create)

In Step 2 you will *get financially naked* by giving every pound a purpose and planning with conscious intentions. You will step into your life's vision, your life's purpose.

Write these three statements down - I want them to become the first mantras that will help guide you on this path:

1. *Get financially naked*
2. *Give every pound a purpose*
3. *Plan with conscious intentions*

Many get stuck at this stage, for two reasons. First: we are not equipped for dealing with the emotions that come up when we lay our finances bare. Second: most of us were never taught how to! A combination of poor financial knowledge and low self-awareness creates the ostrich syndrome effect - we bury our heads in the sand or pass on the responsibility to others.

Get Financially Naked is all about understanding your numbers and beginning to implement your plan. Basing your plan on your current unique relationship with money will ensure that it sticks, and that you will follow it with ease.

Money is just money - a physical thing - paper, quick, neutral. Money itself has no physical or emotional dimension. It's like a cup of tea ...

it's what we feel when we drink the tea that makes a difference (anyone else now fancy an English cuppa?!) It's the same with money.

Step 3 - Future (Grow)

In Step 3 - the *growth* stage - you will focus on your vision, your values, the change you want to create and how to continue momentum and focus. Once you have a sense of where you're going you will implement frequent money dates to ensure you check in with both sides of the coin - emotional and practical - making the necessary tweaks weekly, even daily.

These steps are not linear. They are fluid and interchangeable. They interconnect with and affect each other. When you feel more deserving of wealth you create more wealth, and what often comes with that is another layer of limiting beliefs that needs clearing. At the same time, when you feel better about something you're more likely to take action, more likely to stick to your decisions and behaviours.

THE LEVELS OF WEALTH CREATION

Wealth, when grown emotionally and practically, can be done so with four phases of wealth creation in mind. One way of looking at this is through the lens of *Maslow's Hierarchy of Needs*. The Middle Eastern origin of the word 'wealth' means *happiness and prosperity in abundance of possessions or riches*. It isn't just about money or how much you have in your bank account. It's about how you feel about them. It's about *wellbeing*. When you're stressed about money, you're stressed about other areas of your life. Taking wealth in its purest form means focusing on the *range* of your wellbeing.

The four levels:

1. Financial Insecurity

2. Financial Security

3. Financial Growth

4. Financial Freedom

Maslow's Hierarchy of Needs looks like this:

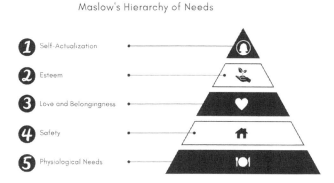

We can place our first level - *Financial Insecurity* - on Maslow's first layer - *Physiological needs*. This represents the basic needs required to survive. Are *your* basic needs met? Or are you just existing? At this level you shouldn't be concerned with investing in the stock market.

Your priority, alongside survival, could be to work towards having a financial security fund, an emergency fund for those times we might call worst case scenarios. *Financial Insecurity* sits at the foundation of wealth creation. Building on that stage will help you to move up to the next stage.

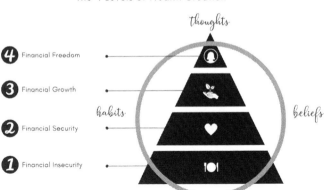

The 4 Levels of Wealth Creation

Our second level - *Financial Security* - sits around Maslow's own second stage - *Safety needs.* If by now you have that emergency fund, is it big enough for anything that could threaten the security you've built? If you're employed, you might benefit from sick pay if your health suffers. What if you are self-employed? Do you have insurance to protect your income to maintain that security?

Our third level - *Financial Growth* - can be placed with Maslow's third stage - *Belongingness and love needs.* You've made it past survival and you have an emergency fund. Remember ... wellbeing is not all about the size of your bank balance. Fulfilling this level is about creating more *time* freedom - time to live the quality of life you deserve, because whilst you need a certain amount of money to exist, you may also need a certain amount of money to enjoy time with your friends and family.

Maslow's fourth level is *Esteem needs* - at which you acquire skills to promote achievement and wellbeing and find your purpose/mission/values. This level crosses between *Financial Growth* and *Financial Freedom.* Just as Maslow's top stage - *Self-actualisation* - relates to self-fulfilment, *Financial Freedom* is achieved when your money is aligned to your values and the income from your assets that you own exceeds your lifestyle expenses. That could be property income, companies that you own by investing in ownership of these companies (which is really all the stock market actually is) or other assets. It is then what you do with it that matters. You will be at your happiest when you use money for ultimate personal growth and development.

You won't climb the hierarchy in a linear fashion but rather move up and down stages. Often you'll need to re-evaluate the levels needed at foundation level as lifestyle creep comes in and your spending needs change. You aren't falling back, you're simply strengthening your foundations.

When I was starting my journey to getting out of debt I wanted all of the levels! I wanted stability but I wanted to feel like I was creating an impact. I was trying to give equal importance to all areas and I failed. The thing is, prioritising all areas means you'll prioritise no areas with any depth and you won't stick to them so none of them become a priority.

Why does this happen? Because we are so often focused on creating more money thinking that *more money* is the solution. How often have you found that that pay rise gets spent or that surge of clients into your business doesn't solve the cash flow challenges? Or we focus on everybody else - Mr and Mrs Jones! We compare ourselves to others because we seek validation and ultimately self-worth and love. Money is often driven by two things. A need for love or a need for status. We want to be seen as someone who cares for others or someone who has it all so that more people will, yep you've guessed it, love us! We give money a lot of power that is often achievable if we just stay focused on our sense of self, our sense of belonging.

As you go through these stages one by one you will build resilience muscles, resilience that will be useful for those times you find yourself slipping back due to circumstances beyond your control. Maslow talks about what motivates us to go from stage to stage and it boils down to values, purpose, mission, goals and also those times we find ourselves rocked by unexpected events.

Which stage are you at right now? What's motivating you to either stay there or progress up to the next level? If your goals are more focused on your values than the pounds, there is more likelihood of achieving them. Look forward to a time when you begin to align your behaviours and emotions to your values and goals, because that's the sweet spot ... that's when you're financially happy *and* have overall wellbeing in your life.

'You wouldn't worry so much about what others think of you if you realized how seldom they do.'

— ELEANOR ROOSEVELT

CHAPTER 1
DESERVE

I f we don't *feel* good enough we fear that we won't *have* enough.

When I was just six years old, my mother pulled me out of my first primary school because the teachers told her they did not allow competitiveness in the school. I was frequently raising my hand in class to answer Miss Hart's questions. I remember feeling the stretching of my hand as I flung it higher and higher into the air to get her attention, being ignored, being told to 'put your hand down. Let someone else speak'. I learned as a young child that I didn't matter. What I had to say did not matter - my model of the world and speaking out was not permitted. I had to remain silent.

It was not surprising that I found speaking my truth in later years somewhat difficult. My understanding was that speaking out was wrong, and so asking for help when I was in financial difficulty was also wrong.

This was a *trauma* ...with a little 't'. My brain perceived that I was not worthy to speak out and be heard. It catalogued that experience as a threat, something to avoid. The brain's main job is to keep you safe, away from pain. The next time I experienced an opportunity to speak, my brain reminded me to stay quiet so that I didn't feel that pain/shame again. This, of course, was only my perception. Our perceptions become our thoughts and our thoughts become our reality. We go on to make decisions based on these perceptions, these traumas.

What is a *money trauma?*

Remember - a trauma is a disruption to the nervous system. It is the body's response to a situation that feels threatening to our sense of safety. A trauma occurs when we are unable to process events and experiences because we lack the tools, emotional/psychological maturity or support system needed. So we store them in the body as *open case files.* These experiences remain in our energy fields and alter our nervous systems, emotional responses and behaviour. Every time we're triggered, these traumas come to the surface. We re-experience them and behave in the same way that the part of us that experienced a similar trauma behaved. This keeps us in a trauma loop and makes it hard for us to choose different response patterns, sometimes leading to physical or mental illness.

Every experience we have as children, particularly during the imprinting period between the age of 0-6 years old, forms our core beliefs.

When it comes to money, we often see a misalignment between our beliefs and what is actually true. *Trauma* is at play when we act from an emotional, irrational state. This shows up in many guises but often in the form of:

- Anxiety
- Depression
- Insomnia
- Shame
- Fear
- Guilt
- Anger
- Perfectionism

- Imposter syndrome
- Lack of empathy
- Procrastination
- Not feeling worthy
- Lack of trust in others
- Chronic disorganisation

These conditions are heightened when part of us wants to feel safe. They are not logical. They are protectors. They try to soothe and distract us from what our brains perceive to be dangerous.

We might therefore:

- Make poor decisions;
- Make decisions based on an emotional response;
- Never get ahead with money or always just make ends meet;
- Fail to stick to the plan we've been given or created;
- Avoid making decisions at all, bury our heads in the sand.
- Pass financial responsibility onto someone else
- Undercharge for our services
- Never get started

In the field of psychology, *cognitive dissonance* occurs when a person holds contradictory beliefs, ideas or values and experiences psychological stress when participating in an action that goes against one or more of them.

When our beliefs are challenged, or when our behaviour is not aligned with our beliefs, a disagreement or *dissonance* is created. The uncomfortable feelings that ensue might manifest as stress, anxiety, regret, shame, embarrassment or feelings of negative self-worth. Trauma combined with the misalignment of values and experiences is a recipe for financial poverty.

If you think about it, we have a lot of cognitive distortions when it comes to money – a lot of 'should' statements - 'I should be good with money.' 'I should be making more money.' 'I should have started investing 10 years ago.'

We *become* the distortion. We make this negative behaviour about ourselves. We make debt our identity - 'I have debt, therefore I am bad' ... *I am bad* versus *I have done something bad*. This is the difference between guilt and shame, which we will look at later.

We need to separate money from our sense of self.

Behind every financial decision we make is a need to feel something. To feel secure and feel valued. By increasing your life net worth and settling your emotional balance sheets ... by establishing new beliefs, new language, new money narratives, new behaviours, new positive emotions around money - you'll be taking steps on your path to financial growth, freedom and 'enoughness'.

But first, what is 'enoughness'?

CHAPTER 2
LEVELS OF ENOUGHNESS

- Not enoughness
- Enoughness
- More than enoughness

S ounds obvious, I know. You simply operate your beliefs and behaviours from one of these levels. They underpin your money story. If you come from *not enoughness*, your story is one of fear and scarcity. If it's *enoughness,* it's comfort and security. *More than enoughness* leads to financial freedom and independence. Your relationship with money is at the core of everything.

So ... how do you really feel about money?

Write down your current yearly salary/income:

To be happier, how much more would you need to earn?

Can you see? Regardless of your starting point, your *Level of Enoughness*, even when you change the numbers, the story remains the same. Relating money to love, for example, will not work. It will never be enough. No amount of money will achieve a sense of 'good enoughness'. The meaning you give to money has power over the worth or unworthiness you create for yourself and go on to make decisions about in your life. In truth, you need to separate who you are from what you have. And if the meaning you give to money is linked to how you feel about your deservedness then the amount of money you receive or give will always be limited by your sense of self.

What are you really seeking when you desire more money? If money didn't exist, what would you want more of?

And don't get me on to the issues of poor financial literacy and lack of financial education in schools. These absolutely keep us stuck in a state of fear and *not enoughness*. Add personal experiences to these - like divorce, grief, redundancy, trauma - layered over time and imprinting themselves. Children should be taught from a young age that money itself is not the taboo subject. It's the *emotions* that are taboo. Who likes talking about guilt? Shame? Fear? Who likes feeling they might be judged?

We imprison ourselves with money shame for longer than criminals serve jail sentences! Our money narratives, the stories and messages we tell ourselves, keep us stuck. We label ourselves as 'bad with money' or 'bad at maths' or 'terrible at managing money' and the underlying shame and guilt holds us prisoner.

This can show up in different ways. We:

- dishonour our own boundaries by allowing others to take our time, make decisions for us or do something that feels misaligned with our values
- undercharge for our services
- overdeliver in our businesses and fall into servitude mode
- endure unhealthy relationships
- place other people's needs before our own.

When we don't feel deserving, we are not able to receive freely.

Once you start working on your relationship with money, you can begin to absorb the rest - financial literacy and the practical steps to financial freedom. It's important to do this outside of the realm of traditional financial advice because that's focused on the solution. We may think we have solutions to our money problems, but there is no point in going straight to the solution, the product or the plan if we don't understand our relationship with money. You can get your trainers out and tell yourself you're going to the gym five times a week, but that's focusing on the solution. Unless you focus on how you feel and how internally motivated you are, your gym attendance will be short-lived. You can promise yourself you'll start that diet tomorrow. Tomorrow comes and you're low in energy, or can't walk past the chocolate biscuits or the wine in the fridge - and the new habit doesn't even get started. You'll self-sabotage, you won't follow the plan, you'll make poor decisions - often based on limiting beliefs (*I'm not the fit type … it never works for me anyway*) - and, worst of all, you are, once again, full of fear, guilt and shame. We focus on the behaviour when we should be starting way back - with how we *think*. How we think affects how we feel, and how we feel drives our behaviours. As the emotions we attach to money change, the way we handle money will change. What is a limiting belief? A Limiting belief is simply a belief that we believe to be an absolute truth. Our brains remind us of these beliefs based upon our perceptions and experiences. These limiting beliefs limit us somehow. They prevent us from living our life without any expectation of a fear of success or a fear of failure. Often when they do limit us, we find that we feel challenged and we head straight to the solution that then leads us to the 'should do's'. Financial educators are often 'shoulding on us'. Your investment portfolio 'should be like this', your credit score 'should be like that'.

The first step, then, is forgiveness.

CHAPTER 3
FORGIVENESS AND SELF WORTH

*W**hat or who do you need to forgive?***
We all have money stuff from our past that needs to be acknowledged, accepted, released and forgiven.

> *'Practising forgiveness means letting go of self-righteous anger, blame and resentment. That's hard. The combination of self righteous anger, blame and resentment is one of my favorites. Umm. Umm. Umm. Drink it up! Unfortunately, I think it's toxic and eats you alive from the inside. It might go down like a milkshake, but it burns up your insides like battery acid.'*
>
> **— BRENÉ BROWN**

I remember the day I realised that my lack of net-worth was wrapped up in my lack of self-worth. I was 27 and living in Jersey. Whilst walking to work at the bank along the windy coastline of St Helier, I stopped by the coffee shop I visited every day. At the counter I saw a white leaflet with the words *Declutter your wardrobe*. I remember laughing with myself at the fun a personal stylist would have with the volume of clothes stacked in my closet. I tucked the leaflet in my bag and that evening casually mentioned to my fiancé how much I would adore a personal styling session for my birthday. He went ahead and booked the stylist and she spent the day weeding out my wardrobe, helping me choose clothes to suit my body shape and make-up to complement my skin tone. We barely scratched the surface on the first visit so I invited her back to work on my other wardrobes. After the second visit I sat on our little red couch surrounded by bin bags of clothes … and cried. I'd been given permission to get rid of all the 'stuff' I'd been hoarding in an attempt to feel better about myself. It changed my life and saved me from a continued spiral of financial poverty.

I had deep money shame. I had to forgive people in my life who had passed that shame to me by the way they treated me growing up. This was the beginning, the start of healing my relationship with money, my relationship with myself.

Activity: *What do you need to forgive?*

What financial decisions do you need to forgive in order to release yourself from the prison of guilt, shame, regret and responsibility?

CHAPTER 4

LOOKING BACK TO LOOK FORWARD

I n order to forgive, we have to first let go of decisions we consider to be bad so that we can feel free to look forwards. By now, you know which stage of the path from *not enoughness* to *more than enoughness* you're at. Now is the time to bring some curiosity to why/how you're at that stage - in essence, your money story.

To begin thinking about your relationship with money it's important to identify the emotions, behaviours, habits and beliefs that underpin it - your *financial past*. I know that for many of you just the word 'money' is emotional and conjures up so much - perhaps guilt, shame, fear, anxiety ... perhaps happiness. The way we spend money and the way we save it is reflected in the way we give and receive, in what we value, what we believe we deserve and have permission to achieve and what we believe is possible for ourselves to experience.

And so - your relationship with money is absolutely about mindset. We rely very much on our internal belief system - it guides us, it influences our decisions, our views, our actions. Being in the wrong mindset can create havoc with our lives and lead to decisions and actions that don't serve us. Having spent most of my teenage years starving myself and overspending on clothes to fill a void, I know what it feels like to be stuck in the wrong mindset. In order to understand your relationship with money, you must uncover it. To do that you must uncover your beliefs. And the easiest place to start is the present day.

Activity: *Think about the following:*

What do I believe about money today?
What meaning am I giving money?
What does having more money mean to me?
What is my biggest fear around money?
What stories am I telling myself that are keeping me stuck?

Check in with some money memories of the past:
How did I treat money growing up?
What was my parents' relationship with money?
Who brought money into the household?
Who do I need to forgive?

Big questions! Don't worry if you can't answer them fully right now ... come back to them as you go through this book and see how your responses change.

One thing we do is to allow our *self-worth* to define our *net-worth*. I repeat: we *allow our self-worth to define our net-worth*. And vice-versa. However, what we have in our bank accounts does not quantify what we're worthy of. I know people who are equally the poorest and loveliest people ... and I know some who are the wealthiest and loveliest people.

People say 'charge your worth'. This is flawed. If your self-worth is low, you won't ever charge enough. We need to separate money from our sense of self.

Understanding your worth is more about knowing what you will bring to the world.

Working on how I feel about myself and understanding my relationship with money has transformed my life over the last few years. Shifting my perspective on money, what it means to me and my worthiness around it resulted in my income growing and my financial situation changing out of all recognition. Your self-worth and self-empowerment are everything. Once you begin to increase both, your confidence will build and you'll be able to do anything. If you had told me five years ago that I'd be speaking on Radio 4 *Woman's Hour* or standing on speaker stages in front of hundreds of people, I'd have said there is no way I'd have the confidence ... but you all know that a confident woman can rule the world, and what I achieved is entirely possible for all of *you*, whatever your hopes, dreams, aspirations. Whatever you want to do, you are entirely capable as a strong woman to do those things.

I see a lot of female entrepreneurs, in particular, who display a lack of self-worth in their ability. They think 'If I just buy another course, pass another qualification, read another book, I'll have the confidence to charge more for my services, take the next step or do the next thing in my business'. They're afraid to ask for help, to have belief in their ability and what they can achieve. They feel they have to do more. But there's a difference between investing in yourself because you want to learn and doing it because you feel like you're not good enough.

Money is about three things: how comfortable you feel to receive, to retain and how comfortable you feel to give. Receiving money comfortably requires vulnerability. It requires you to pause what you are doing and allow someone or something in. To allow money to flow. In order to receive, there must be room for expansion. This means allowing yourself to be supported, loved, given to, valued, paid money in exchange for your services or goods. In order to retain, we need to feel deserving to keep hold of it.

One of the fastest ways to get better at receiving money is to practise being more generous with yourself. Yes, that's right - to give more to yourself in priority over others. This is not about the amount of money you give to yourself - in fact, the gift of time may be more valuable to you. We often value our time far less, which is crazy. It is the one asset we cannot create more of in life!

Give yourself more. More time to sleep, more time to read, more time to meander around your favourite childhood town, more time to drink your favourite drink twice as slowly as you normally would.

Let's create a sense of more than enoughness. A state of sufficiency. Don't get by with just enough. Don't stay in an unconscious pattern of just enoughness. Expand your deserved-ness.

(I share a weekly 15-minute practice I use in my daily life to help you stretch this comfort zone in the *Grow* section later in this book).

CHAPTER 5
THE EMOTIONS OF MONEY

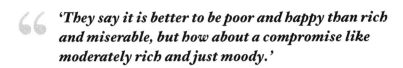

'They say it is better to be poor and happy than rich and miserable, but how about a compromise like moderately rich and just moody.'

— **PRINCESS DIANA**

I n order to *Step into wealth*®, we have to feel wealthy before we become wealthy. There is little logic in most of the decisions we make about money. They come from how we feel, hence why people get into debt cycles, go bankrupt or don't take enough risks. Think about the meaning and power we give to money and the emotions wrapped up in that. These are some phrases shared by people I've worked with:

It's more important to give to others than myself.

It's better to give than to receive.

I want doesn't get.

If you're a good person and do the right thing then money will take care of itself.

*People who want & spend money on themselves are
frivolous/selfish/materialistic.*

Money doesn't grow on trees.

In for a penny, in for a pound.

It's hard to make money.

There will never be enough.

You can only have the lifestyle you want by planning and being careful.

There will always be enough money.

There's more where that came from.

Don't worry, something will come up, it always does.

My partner takes care of the money.

Money just isn't important to me.

Some key human emotions come out of these money narratives: a
sense of responsibility; a feeling of shame or unworthiness; a feeling
of guilt; a sense of regret for previous decisions. What are the
consequences of holding onto these emotions? Have you ever lost
sleep over money? Have you suffered stress from not having enough?
Money is one of the biggest causes of stress and divorce in this
country - stress built on fear. Ironically, 'fear' as an acronym could be
False Evidence Appearing Real. It's not real, is it? What we fear only
appears real. Fear, instead, is just an emotion. You may have
experienced fear that turned out to be unfounded, and when you did
the thing you were afraid of, the fear disappeared. In truth, you are
100% capable of managing your own money and managing your
emotions around money, and when these two things come together,
it's magic.

As women, though, we lack confidence. We procrastinate and we
hide. We have good intentions, and then the fear sets in. But there is
no point in tackling the practical aspects of money management if

you still have fear. Tackle the emotion first: fear, anxiety, apprehension, feeling that you should look after everybody else before yourself, feeling guilty if you spend money on yourself, or, conversely, overspending because you're trying to fill a void; shame, embarrassment, worry, pride, not understanding, feeling there is too much paperwork, too many figures, a lack of trust, urgency, anxiety, fear of making the wrong decision, doubt, excitement, confusion, overwhelm, worry, suspicion of advice, urgency, confusion. I could go on. And the chemical release of those emotions will make its presence known in your body. Pay attention to that ... be aware of where it kicks in when you're triggered into fight or flight mode. Most will feel it in their stomach, chest or throat - the three main chakras of the body. Identify where you store yours because doing so is likely to be physically damaging.

The stomach is our second brain. People talk about going with your gut, feeling in your gut, trusting your gut.

First - what *is* the emotion? What does it look like? Feel like? Where are you storing it? Knowing all of this exposes the emotion for what it is - just an emotion. It is not *who* you are. Next - acknowledge that money itself doesn't create that emotion. Money is just a tool. The cause of the emotion is created by the meaning we have attached to it.

Consider also - does this emotion come from an external judgement of what other people might be thinking about you right now or does it come from your own internal judgement?

CHAPTER 6
GUILT AND SHAME

G uilt, as per Wikipedia, is *an emotional experience that occurs when a person believes or realises, accurately or not, that they have compromised their own standards of conduct or have violated universal moral standards and bear significant responsibility for that violation.*

Shame, as per Wikipedia, is *an unpleasant self-conscious emotion typically associated with a negative evaluation of the self; withdrawal motivations; and feelings of distress, exposure, mistrust, powerlessness, and worthlessness.*

Guilt and shame are not the same. Guilt is when you feel bad about a negative impact you've had on others. Shame is evoked when you let yourself down or don't live up to your own sense of what is right.

Shame can often show up when we talk about money and connect it to our sense of self with the words 'I am':

'I am bad with money.'

'I am no good at budgeting.'

'I am an overspender and no good at managing money.'

Staying stuck in the patterns of shame leads to money avoidance ... you avoid making decisions, you avoid looking at bank statements, and so create more shame and avoidance. And more avoidance = postponement or lack of decision-making.

When I was a practising financial adviser I saw money shame come up every single day, e.g. one partner in the money conversation not wanting to speak; the people who returned into their overdraft six months after arranging a debt consolidation loan for them; the person who received an inheritance or lottery win and within 12 months had spent all the money because they feared the responsibility of keeping it or giving it away, and the guilt of receiving and holding onto it.

Jemma's story: Jemma came from a wealthy background. Her guilt around the privilege she experienced led to overgiving to others in order to feel safe from judgement. She related the wealth she received from her father to love. 'I can't have love and be independently wealthy' she said in our first meeting. Together we worked towards an understanding that by putting her own needs before others' was not selfish but, in fact, enriching and would help Jemma to develop a more relaxed attitude to risk, particularly in relationships.

W hose shame are you carrying? Financial shame comes up when we feel we're not living up to someone else's expectations or ideals. We measure ourselves by what we perceive others' lives to be.

> *'Shame is the intensely painful feeling or experience of believing that we are flawed and therefore unworthy of love and belonging — something we've experienced, done, or failed to do makes us unworthy of connection.'*
>
> — **BRENE BROWN**

I grew up believing like many of you that all debt was bad. You didn't borrow what you couldn't pay back. You didn't spend what you didn't have. At school, if a number was a negative you needed to find the right sum to turn it back into a positive. If I went into an overdraft on my bank statement, it showed in red on the screen. Society decreed that you must 'stay in the black'.

When I was 15 my dad and twin brother emigrated to Australia. Part of me was incredibly excited for them and the new opportunities they would create for themselves. However, I couldn't help feeling abandoned. The inner child in me felt unloved. Surely - if I was good enough, they wouldn't leave? If I was worthy of love they would stay? My brain, my unconscious mind, was telling me that as long as I continued to hold onto these emotions, I'd be safe. And so it looked for more and more evidence to back that up, to remind me that the cycles of behaviour I was following - later, the cycle of debt - were keeping me safe.

The irony is that fear, guilt and shame DO serve to protect us in many ways. Think about a time that you were scared of something - perhaps a fairground ride or crossing a busy road. That kind of fear protects you. Other fears will block you, stop you from doing something.

I went into postnatal depression and PTSD after we nearly lost my youngest son Thomas because I felt that I should have known he was sick. I felt guilty as a mother and massively anxious. I tried to control everything in my life including my son's routine, my friendships and my relationship with money. I could not control that my son had been so ill and so I went into a whirlwind of overspending to protect myself.

It sounds terrible and it was ... but seemingly negative emotions - fear, guilt, shame - can serve a positive purpose. Serious life challenges - illness, redundancy, mental health issues - for you or somebody close can have a huge impact on your relationship with money. There are times we're not in the right space to let go of those emotions - they actually protect us - and it serves us to consider when would be the best time to do so. Think about how the brain is able to take past trauma out of your memory bank and into your unconscious. You might not even remember certain things until something triggers them. Only you will know when it's the right time to let go.

CHAPTER 8
REGRET AND ANGER

R egret, as per Wikipedia, is *the emotion of wishing one had made a different decision in the past, because the consequences of the decision were unfavourable.*

Regret is terrible, but take solace from the fact that you did what felt right at the time with the resources you had. Consider what you would do differently next time. Step back into your power!

We need to forgive *ourselves* for bad decisions in order to recognise that sometimes they're there to protect us. I'm sure I overspent in my twenties to protect myself, because if I didn't do that, what else would I have done? When I was 15 or 16 I basically stopped eating for about eight years on and off and then started overspending. If I hadn't changed my behaviour from under eating to overspending, I can't bear to think what would have happened. It served me ... and there will be situations where you have just had to do what you've had to do to survive, get out of debt, avoid bankruptcy. Whatever you did, you did it for a reason - and now it's time to forgive yourself for that decision. That emotion, that decision, is not *who* you are. Let me say that again - that decision you made in the past is not who you are now.

Perhaps forgiveness needs to happen for a financial decision you made when it was the only decision you could have made to get through the situation you were in? Perhaps it's time to draw that line in the sand and forgive yourself?

My husband and I bought a house in 2007 just before the markets crashed. We were both working in mortgages at the time, so felt fairly comfortable with how mortgages work and not overstretching ourselves. So what did we do? We overstretched ourselves.

We took an unsecured loan out to pay for legal fees. Our parents asked if we were sure it was a wise move but we were so driven on wanting this house that we just ignored everything around us. And then the markets crashed and we ended up selling that property seven or eight years later for the amount we purchased it for - and felt terrible. My husband often said afterwards that he would never make that decision again. In effect, he was storing that bad decision in his unconscious belief system ... and that belief system was telling him 'You are not good with money'. In fact, my husband is very good with money ... it was just a really unlucky decision. Markets crash. There was nothing we could have done about that, and we were most certainly not the only couple this had happened to. Eventually we had to openly forgive ourselves for that decision. We learned from it. We learned how we would do things differently going forward. Again, those emotions - guilt, shame, fear - they are not who you are. You are not that shame. You are not Mrs Guilt. You are you. You are beautiful. You don't have to become that emotion. You just need to feel it.

Anger and regret are connected. Anger relates to our perception of the control we have over our environment. The more control we perceive, the less angry we are likely to feel when something happens. When we feel in control of our money, our sense of personal power increases. Holding on to anger, therefore, will make us feel disempowered with money. We feel frustrated, entitled, that we should have more money and that things are happening *to* us rather than *for* us or *because of* us.

Emotions need motion in order to shift. The *Money Narratives Clearing*® method, which I will introduce you to in this book, has a vitally important step within it - acknowledging that every emotion we feel serves a purpose. It may not be the purpose you want or seek for you to make better decisions with money, but they serve to protect you away from harm and towards happiness. What would happen if you were able to look upon these emotions as positive messages telling you that you're safe and telling you more about yourself, more about who you are? What are these messages telling you about the lessons you've learned? What are they telling you about what you believe in passionately? About how you could use money to create a more positive impact for the world?

It is time to let go.

Your relationship with savings is as important, if not more so, than your relationship with debt. Back in my twenties I ignored my unhealthy relationship with money and focused on building up savings to pay off my debts. There is a big mindset shift from focusing on moving *away* from having less (debt) versus the abundance mindset of moving *towards* having more (savings). If you simply pay off debts, you're likely to return to them because you haven't developed a new habit to replace the old one. You'll continue those patterns of negativity and not enoughness. If you focus on creating and reinforcing a new positive savings habit, you will move forward towards a future full of hope, opportunity and prosperity (more on debt later in the *Create* stage).

Financial experts will often tell you to focus on paying off the debts first, and there is some logic to this. High interest debts can lead to prolonged debt cycles and more debts. But what this doesn't take into account is the impact of remaining in a mindset of not enoughness, which can play havoc with our personal relationships and our wellbeing, both emotional and physical. It can prevent us from contributing our time, energy and money towards tasks that we value most, time with our families and our communities.

One of the most common reasons for getting into debt is having insufficient money set aside in savings to dip into when needed. It becomes a cycle. Perhaps the credit card has been paid off but then the car tyre bursts or the washing machine breaks down. With no savings, debt builds again.

Shifting your mindset and practical steps towards making savings a priority will change your financial future.

Begin with small steps. When I was in this position, I did two things. I switched my bank account so that I could reset my balance to zero. I set up a standing order to pay off my overdraft each month. I created a spending plan and I gave every pound a purpose. My new awareness of my spending habits enabled me to begin saving for the non-fixed expenses. I started with a few hundred pounds and soon my mindset began to shift from one of *not enoughness* to *enoughness* to *more than enoughness*. With less motivation to spend on impulsive items, I planned more consciously and mindfully, and with alignment to my financial values.

How much money you save is about the life you want to live, the purpose you choose to give money, the meaning you choose to give it. You've got this.

How to uncover the emotion behind spending

Activity: *Grab a piece of paper and write down your answers to these questions*:

Think of a time when you last spent money. How did you feel? Bored, stressed, lonely, happy, excited?
What were you doing just before? Had you just done something stressful? Had you just had an argument with somebody?
Why did you feel the need to buy this item?

What need would it fulfil? How else could this have been met? Are there certain things that trigger your spending? Did you really need it? What could you have spent it on instead?

How did you feel after you bought it? Was it a temporary release of emotion? Was it long-lasting?

The aim with these questions is to bring awareness and challenge your emotions from past decisions so that you are more informed and empowered to deal with them again in the future. By being curious to negative thoughts you will learn more about your emotional needs. If you can change how you feel, you can change your behaviour.

Money itself, then, is not the cause. Something else causes the negativity and creates the impulse. Find that. Don't always beat up that inner critic - sometimes it's there to protect you.

Emotions are not bad. They serve a purpose to give us information and to protect us from pain and hurt.

Things you can do when emotions come up around money:

1. Take a deep breath in for three and out for six. This tells your nervous system that you are safe.

2. Acknowledge the emotion.

3. Thank it for keeping you safe.

4. Separate the fact from the fiction - what is actually true here?

5. Ask yourself what it's telling you.

6. Identify an emotion you can use to counterbalance it.

Allow the emotions to *empower* you, not *disempower* you.

CHAPTER 9
RESPONSIBILITY

Financial dependence can lead to low self-esteem and self-worth and is often linked to having been financially rescued by a spouse or parent. The money may come with strings attached, resulting in resentment towards the giver. Historically, women have been financially dependent on men because of the gender pay gap and/or having children to care for. If you are a woman reading this book, start thinking now about how you will create financial independence for yourself, not as an exit strategy from your relationship, but in order to become financially responsible.

Financial independence is a relatively new concept for women in a country where women have only been permitted to take out their own mortgages since 1982. We're still getting used to the novelty of going out to work, earning our own living, managing our own finances and having our own choices - to be part of a family or go it alone; to be employed or be our own boss. It's understandable that we're still grappling with the conflicts these choices present. We grapple with our sense of identity and self-worth and the ideas of asserting our value and building wealth.

Women no longer have to feel culturally or socially obliged to be in a relationship and it's true to say that there are enormous challenges in managing your finances with someone else. If it goes wrong, generally speaking, the woman will come out worse. We are way behind in terms of women's long-term wealth building. We're not as informed or confident as we should be. This is about you being *ind*ependent, not *co*-dependent.

Here are some tips to start creating financial independence for yourself:

1. Understand the money in your household even if you are not the one managing it.
2. Have money in your own name for accessibility and to make your own decisions, independent of your partner.
3. Save a little each month into a 'giving' pot to treat yourself without any guilt attached.
4. Invest in your future self rather than rely on your partner's future income (more on this in the *Grow* section).
5. Put your needs as high as others'. Create a list of your future desires.

 'A woman needs money and a room of her own if she is to be able to write.'

— **VIRGINIA WOLFE**

If you have children, think about how you can help them to develop their own sense of freedom with money. You may think that financially rescuing them when they are in difficulty is the right thing to do, for instance, but in the long term this can create a sense of co-dependency with money. *Financial enabling* is help that hurts. The underlying emotion that leads a parent to rescue their child financially is often deep-rooted guilt. Money is used to fill an unmet emotional need from childhood. The parent that lived in poverty growing up may not want their child to want for anything. They won't want them to feel the same pain. Bailing them out is a protection strategy.

When you're about to make a gift to your children, ask yourself if that gift will help or hinder them. Helping them out with their education, for example, is different from paying off the credit card debt they've built up by overspending. Rescuing them won't help them change their behaviours.

Here are my top 10 tips for helping children develop a positive relationship with money:

1 – Set limits

Appreciating the value of patience over instant gratification is a great lesson for children. In a world where so much is on demand, setting limits on technology, for instance, will help them develop the skill of waiting.

2 – Acts of kindness

A balanced relationship with money is crucial, and a balance of spontaneity, planning, fun, giving, status, being carefree will make for a healthy relationship. Acts of kindness - not necessarily with money ... it could be with time, for example - will teach children the value of what they're giving. And don't forget, children often mirror your behaviour. If *you're* giving, often they will mirror that.

3 – Enforce consequences

Sometimes it's useful for children to feel a little uncomfortable with their emotions. Of course, we don't want them to feel pain, but they have to feel pain to feel pleasure. They have to understand disappointment. The knowledge that they can't have everything can help prevent getting into bad debt as adults.

4 – Do things together

The little things you do with your kids can make a massive difference. Food shopping is a great one. You can teach kids so much when you're food shopping, even concepts like the *Fridge, Freezer and Larder* approach to money management that we'll look at later in this book. Maybe you could have a conversation about how to shave £20 off this week's food bill and put that money towards a fun fund.

5 – Talk openly about money

This is so important. How many of you grew up with money secrets in the house? Did your parents hide conversations about money? Did they never talk about it? Talking openly about money is really important. For example, if you need to make an insurance claim, get them involved. Teach them the importance of insurance to cover emergencies. It will help them to learn to look after their things and also remove fear and anxiety around things going wrong.

Talk about car insurance renewal. Ask if you should pay up front or in monthly instalments? Talk to them about the differences between both.

6 - Allow them to make their own decisions

I remember being seven or eight at a caravan park in France with my three brothers and sisters and step-brother and sister. My step-dad gave us £5 each to go to the shop and buy whatever we wanted for dinner. It's the only clear memory I have of being given money to make a decision about. I bought a pot noodle and absolutely loved it! My brothers came up with the clever idea that if we clubbed together we could buy something a bit nicer. I was having none of it. This was my decision!

It's interesting that this memory has stuck with me. Being granted the responsibility to make decisions must have made a real impression on me.

7 – Reward positive money behaviours

Just as an employer matches pension contributions, how about matching every pound your child saves (within reason)?

8 – Teach them that debt can be used

Teach them that debt is not always bad, but can be used cautiously. Many of you will have come across Martin Lewis and his work on good debt and bad debt. University fees are *good* debt. Investing in your business can be good debt.

9 – Teach them how to be responsibly spontaneous

My relationship with money has always been spontaneous, right from the first pound I earned putting letters in envelopes and posting them for my dad's business. My next job was picking asparagus in the depths of winter. It was horrendous, but when I received my pay I would spend it immediately because I had this fear that if I didn't spend it somebody else would. I also felt like if I had nice things, more people would like me. When I look back, I can see that spontaneity is not necessarily a sign of a negative relationship with money. I can see how it serves me, too. The fact that I'm spontaneous with a lot of things means that I take risks and get things done. Others may need to plan and then find the implementation difficult because the spontaneity isn't there. Teaching children how to be responsibly spontaneous, responsibly planning, responsibly carefree, responsibly status-driven and responsibly giving in their relationship with money helps to create balance for them.

10 – Ignore everybody else

Ignore everybody else.

It's so important to stay in *your* lane and think about what's important for *you*, nobody else. Nobody else is living your life. You can only do your best.

CHAPTER 10

GENEROSITY, LOVE AND CODEPENDENCY

'*It is better to give than to receive; I prefer to look after other people's needs before my own.*'

How many of you heard this growing up or feel like this about money?

Growing up, many of us are taught that giving is good and taking is bad: *share with your brothers and sisters, give to others in need.* We are rarely taught that giving has boundaries. Giving with no boundaries means that our own needs go unfulfilled. When our own needs are unfulfilled we feel resentment towards others and under appreciated. We then become co-dependent.

One of the signs of codependency is overgiving. When we are codependent we take our sense of self from the act of pleasing others. We are *people-pleasers.* We overgive in order to receive praise and attention and that, in turn, provides a feeling of esteem. But it's ungrounded esteem ... it comes not from within, but from without.

Signs that you may be codependent:

- You feel responsible for other people's problems.
- You feel used and under-appreciated.

- You try to please other people so that they will like you.
- You take things personally.
- You use manipulation, shame or guilt to control the behaviour of others.
- You feel like a victim.
- You lie to yourself and make excuses for others' behaviour.
- You value the approval of others more than you value yourself.
- You ignore your own financial needs.

Overgiving often comes from a deeper need and makes us feel depleted rather than more fulfilled. It becomes a habit. We overgive in an attempt to feel better, but then feel agitated when it isn't reciprocated. Overgiving is often a sign that we wish to assuage our guilt. Many parents I have worked with overgive to their children in order to feel less guilty about something or to release shame from their own childhood. We might overgive because we think we 'should', based on other people's perceptions of us.

Being a people-pleaser can create stress, anxiety and long-term illness. You fear judgement so might avoid mistakes when trying new things. Instead, try to embrace these imperfections. Acknowledge the emotion that the people-pleaser part of you is trying to communicate. Thank her and think about giving yourself permission to focus on you.

You are loved. You are enough.

Ask yourself:

What am I giving by giving away my time or money?

What am I seeking more of by giving to others?

What needs do I have that are unfulfilled?

What boundaries do I have in place to ensure my needs are met?

By avoiding confrontation, what am I actually trying to avoid?

What will be the consequences if I continue to neglect my own needs to attend to others first?

What could I do to focus more on my own needs?

What boundaries do I need to set?

Marcus' story: Marcus came to me in his capacity as a financial professional. He felt a strong link between the way he spent money and a desire to be liked. His behaviours with money were driven by a desire to please others, so he would turn up at client meetings in flash cars and spend money on things that gave him no long-term satisfaction but instead made him feel 'tight and held within.' He felt depleted of energy.

I asked Marcus which part of him was telling him that he wanted to be liked and he said it was the eight-year-old boy. I asked what would be possible for him if he let that people-pleaser go. He responded that the happiest he'd ever been was when he let his ego collapse. He said he'd be able to 'live with freedom' because he would 'not be consciously thinking about what other people thought.' It was a huge lightbulb moment for Marcus.

The emotions that are possible when we let go of the parts of us that are trying to protect us can be life-changing. Marcus was able to feel less fear, have a freer mind and find the courage to give that love to himself.

CHAPTER 11
POWER

Society hasn't done a good job when it comes to women and power. It is as if it isn't feminine or natural for a woman to have wealth.

As a child of divorced parents, I saw how money was used to hold power over another. I recall the hushed family conversations and arguments about how much my father was to give my mother for child maintenance. As a young child I believed the old trope that money was the root of all evil, so as soon as I received it I wanted to get rid of it. The deposit for my first house was scraped together from a car accident payout. Money had bad things associated with it. I didn't want it.

Here are two questions to ponder on:

1. How much power are you giving away to money?
2. Or are you allowing previous memories or experiences to shadow your beliefs?

CHAPTER 12
TRAUMA AND THE 4 TRAUMA RESPONSES

F *ear and the four trauma responses (one I bet you have not heard of!)*

There are three classic responses to fear — *fight, flight* and *freeze*.

When our brains perceive a threat we automatically go into one of these stress response modes. From an evolutionary perspective, these responses have served us by enabling us to respond quickly and get to a place of safety. However, when trauma is involved, the threat never feels like it went away, leaving us stuck in different stress response modes. We become the person who seems to get edgy at the slightest glimpse of provocation (fight), or the highly anxious person who avoids family gatherings (flight), or the individual who procrastinates and feels unable to make any financial decisions (freeze).

Pete Walker, a family therapist and Complex Post Traumatic Stress Disorder Survivor (C-PTSD)[1] coined a fourth state of trauma response - *fawning*. He says:

 'Fawn types seek safety by merging with the wishes, needs and demands of others. They act as if

*they unconsciously believe that the price of
admission to any relationship is the forfeiture of
all their needs, rights, preferences and boundaries.'*

— **PETE WALKER**

Fawning is a trauma response otherwise also known as 'tend and befriend'. It is more common in women; when we feel unsafe or in a trauma-triggered state, we go to a place of fawning - essentially people-pleasing.

Your brain goes into protection mode because its number one job is to keep you safe and to help you survive. When I was trapped in a cycle of hanging my money in my wardrobe with overspending I know now that I was stuck in trauma. I was self-harming. I was trying to please myself and trying to please others in an attempt to feel safe. Remember that trauma is stored in the unconscious mind.

As adults, we are often drawn to relationships that feel comfortable. The brain, therefore, perceives that in order to feel safe we should be the people-pleaser, and so, somebody who has experienced trauma or abuse will please people in order to feel safe:

- saying yes to too many things;
- avoiding financial conflict in relationships;
- overgiving to the detriment of their own needs;
- overgiving their time;
- undervaluing or undercharging.

We have been taught as women that we don't have direct access to power and need to develop very good manipulation skills in order to access it. Or we need to put on the masculine suit so that we can step into masculine power. Many women have moved into a very masculine energy to try and create a historic shift and have lost contact with the empowered feminine energy. When we operate from an over-masculine energy with our finances, it can show up in scenarios like these:

- wanting to be in charge or in control of money;
- thriving off adrenaline and being in constant launch mode to make ever more money, perhaps never feeling like it is enough;
- feeling the need to be financially independent and survive alone;
- suffering from depleted energy and, as a consequence, failing health;
- feeling driven by status and external validation.

Conversely, a woman in high feminine energy can be:

- passive;
- reactive rather than proactive to financial decisions;
- submissive (allowing men to make the financial decisions);
- needy of permission from others.

To be truly empowered around wealth we need to access both the masculine *and* the feminine energy. We need to show money our love *and* confidence whilst managing it effectively.

It could be said that some differences are down to evolution ... men as the hunters and women as gatherers. Men are raised to see the world as a hierarchical and competitive space - there is always a winner and a loser. Women see the world as co-operative and democratic and are inclined to share their possessions and their feelings. Women are allowed to be needy whilst men are discouraged from showing vulnerability. These hierarchical differences can lead to a whole heap of financial power struggles and clashes with financial values.

Look at the difference between the ways the media speaks to men and women. *Starling Bank's* research in their *Make Money Equal* campaign[2] states: '*Men are taught the benefits of blockchain and cryptocurrency. Women are told to give up coffee so they can buy a pair of Louboutins.*' (Starling Bank *Make Money Equal* campaign). The ensuing havoc in the financial bedroom can leave the man feeling inadequate and create power shifts if the woman earns more. Finding ways to level the financial playing field so that each person feels financially valuable in the relationship (regardless of what they earn) is key. Achieving a balance between feminine and masculine energy will lead to a deeper sense of wellbeing and happiness and a better relationship with money for both.

Sue's story: Sue came to me feeling inconsistent around money and fearful about her future. She talked about having a weight of responsibility on her shoulders whilst not bringing sufficient financial value to the family. Money felt hard. Her father had brought in the money when she was growing up and her mother came from a background of not enoughness. Sue began to explore the language used in her household. Her father used to say: 'You have to make your own way' and 'You won't get any inheritance.' From the age of six, the beliefs that her brain took as truth were linked to having to work hard to have enough money. Subsequently, she worked like a trooper for a corporate organisation. She disliked the CEO who was operating in constant masculine energy, and she had a long-term desire to work for herself. Replicating her father's relationship with money, Sue found it easier to give than to receive. She discovered that she was continuing this behaviour around money in an attempt to get his approval. She believed that whenever someone gave her money, there were strings attached. It also came up that she was resistant to switching her bank account because it was opened with her nan and her mum who was very unwell at the time. The emotion she attached to the account prevented her from moving it, despite the logic of knowing that doing so would help her. Sue began to focus on her own financial choices. With love, she gave back the beliefs she'd learned from her father that money was hard to receive but easy to give and took on the beliefs her nan gave her six-year-old self in order to feel empowered to take actions towards transforming her relationship with money. As a consequence, she negotiated a 28% pay rise at work, became debt-free and improved the conversations at home with her partner and children.

———

Activity: *Feminine and masculine energy matrix*

Take a piece of paper and draw a line down the centre. Label one side *Masculine* and the other *Feminine*.

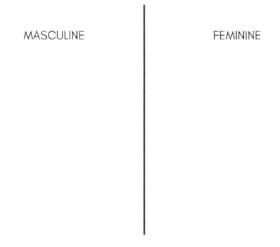

MASCULINE   FEMININE

Think about the feminine and masculine examples you had growing up around money. Who had the biggest influence on you? Was it a man or a woman? What was their energy predominantly? What did they teach you about money? Are you operating from the masculine or feminine energy with how you are treating money?

———

Many men perceive themselves as hunter gatherers. Perhaps they saw their fathers earning the main wage and carry the belief that the man has to be the main income provider. It's always worth trying to understand your partner's operating system so that you can discuss the impact this has on his contribution to the household.

Sue and her partner decided to buy a ceramic chicken and place it in the centre of their table, similar to the TV series *Bread*. Every Sunday during their money date (see *Grow*) they add a non-financial contribution to the pot as a symbol of what they contribute that is not financially dependent. They are free to express both the masculine and feminine energy and the financial and non-financial contribution to the household.

Balance is important in any relationship and money is no exception.

CHAPTER 13
ENERGY

The energy that you have around money is, of course, impacted by your thoughts, emotions and behaviours. With a finite amount of energy to use in your day, energy used on negative emotions is energy wasted. It's crucial to make sure that that energy level is positive.

The thoughts that come from the stories you tell yourself can lead to leaks of your energy, energy required to make shifts in your personal, business or financial life. Think about how long it takes you to move from one task to another. For example, when I go from recording a video to coaching a client, that's a shift, a completely different task involving different skills - and takes up a lot of energy.

If you're using your energy from a *scarcity mindset* perspective, you're wasting energy that could be directed to a mindset of *abundance*. Your unconscious beliefs about money will sabotage your good intentions for the day about creating wealth without you even realising it. Perhaps you dream of growing your business and changing the world, or going for that promotion at work, but then sabotage your success with behaviours that take you off course.

Putting your energy out in a negative way will bring only negativity back. Whatever you put out to the world is actually what you want to attract. If you put love out into the world it's because you want love back. If you put out vibes that reflect your inability to deal with money, it's because you want to be rescued. And that doesn't always end happily, does it? How many people do you know who have been financially rescued by parents, for instance, who think they're doing a good thing? How has it panned out for those people? Rescuing them doesn't teach them how to get out of those cycles themselves or change the underlying behaviour.

It's also important to recognise when you genuinely do need support. Talking therapy didn't work for me and my PTSD. I'm not suggesting it doesn't work for other people, but it kept me stuck in the moment. I then discovered *Rapid Transformational Therapy*[1] - a programme developed by Marissa Peers. It's a combination of *NLP* (neuro linguistic programming) and retraining the brain with behavioural therapy and hypnosis - and that did it for me. I got to the root cause of the problem very quickly and then simply listened to a hypnosis track every night for about four weeks so that it could begin to reset my belief pattern. I believe the best route to help depends on people's personalities. I'm very much an optimist - always have been - so I guess it was easier for me to work on myself because I was always looking at how I could use that pain to help myself and others ... how, for example, I could use it to drive me to launch my podcast, to build my business, to help other people who had been through similar experiences.

To change our results, we have to change that blueprint, that core script, and understand that these beliefs do not serve us.

CHAPTER 14

EMPOWERING MONEY STATEMENT

The way you feel about money is emotional, so practising new feelings will help you to create change. Once you know which emotion you wish to adopt, think about where you will feel this most - perhaps in your stomach, your chest, your throat, your hands. Say: 'I feel loved...' Where do you feel this? Now say: 'I am loved.' Do you feel this in the same place? Close your eyes and repeat this statement of love. If you practise this in a meditative state first you can then use it in the scenario to which you will apply it. When you open your payslip, say: 'I am loved. I feel safe with the amount of money I have earned this month.'

A money mantra will regulate the mind and help to ground you in possibility. Here is how to create one:

1. Create a cue to help you begin, e.g, when brushing your teeth or opening up your bank app.
2. Take a deep breath and clear your mind.
3. Begin with an 'I am' statement, as if you already believe it.
4. State a positive intention that you want to focus on.
5. Make it all sensory - feel, hear, see, touch and taste.
6. Add in some positive emotion.

7. Make it intentional with a clear aim.

Example: *I am feeling positive about my day ahead and I am living it today by gracefully holding my boundaries strong to say no when I need to.*

Activity: *Complete this sentence:*

Money is ... with a mantra that will serve you.

Write it on a piece of paper and put it somewhere you can see it every single day - brushing your teeth, doing your make-up, going to the loo, making a cup of tea. Set it as a screensaver on your phone; write it on your mirror; have it next to your bed.

Repeat that sentence to yourself before you go to sleep and then when you wake up - as many times as possible. You could record yourself saying it on your phone and listen to it every single morning or even set it as your alarm clock. There are many things you can do just to get repeated access to that new belief. Commit to that, and you'll begin to see some real change. You'll see the power of really focusing on your self-worth - because in order to attract more money into your life you need to reject that *scarcity mindset* and embrace that *abundance mindset* ... and *really* believe that it is possible for you.

This is about taking your head out of the sand and accepting responsibility. Your statement could be: 'I'm 100% responsible for my own self-worth around money'. Perhaps it could be: 'I'm capable of making decisions around money'; or 'I'm making decisions around money with confidence'; or 'I'm making decisions about money with the future that I deserve to have'; or 'I deserve to attract more wealth'. The purpose is to create a kind of repeated exposure - a *feedback loop*. And anchoring your new habit to something you do every day is important. If you anchor it to something you're already doing that you don't consciously think about, it can become a new habit that you don't think about. Money likes respect and appreciation. The cumulative effect of those daily thoughts will create long-lasting change for you.

Now congratulate yourself for the small changes you're creating. Remember - small steps = big wins. It will take time for something to become your new money story, and small daily changes will help you to begin taking action and begin living in this new life that you're creating for yourself, this new deservedness around money.

CHAPTER 15
HABITS AND BEHAVIOURS

H abits are harder to break over time because they become increasingly natural to who we are and how we behave. Research shows that we automatically favour what is familiar to us. Your brain doesn't want anything complicated. It will always prefer to follow the flow of what is familiar.

Some spending cycles can become addictions. Dr. Gabor Mate[1], author of *In the Realm of Hungry Ghosts*, defines addiction as 'when we do something over and over again to temporarily decrease pain and increase pleasure in the moment'. The consequences for overspending are that when you pay for something that's out of your budget, it becomes normal to feel that pain, and that pain becomes a recurring pattern.

Continuing to carry that old pain leads to disconnection from the present moment. This leads to a disconnection from self, which is essentially what we call codependency.

Activity: *What old pain are you holding onto that is limiting your ability to give or receive more?*

Carl Jung[2] thought psychological emptiness may be felt as restlessness, a void, or a hunger that can drive addictive behaviour ... the powerlessness of our ego to control our mind. Psychological emptiness is common among codependents, including addicts and individuals with mental health issues. They have difficulty accessing their innate self because their feelings, thinking and behaviour revolve around other people or an addiction. They live externally through the lives of others, whose opinions measure their own worth.

Nikki Myers[3], a yoga therapist, teacher and somatic experiencing practitioner who founded *CITYOGA School of Yoga and Health* launched *Yoga of 12-Step Recovery (Y12SR)* in 2004 based on her own struggles with addiction. She describes codependency as '*The disease of the lost self. We lose connection with ourselves*'.

It's powerful to think about the link between our sense of self and how we feel about money.

CHAPTER 16
CONSUMERISM

You only have to open your phone and browse social media channels to see the impact society has on our relationship with money. Throughout life we might encounter trauma that impacts our sense of self and innate worthiness - divorce, grief, redundancy, ill-health, Covid-19, abuse or self-sabotage. The dark side of consumerism is that when we're at our most vulnerable there will always just happen to be a convenient product or service to ease the pain - the latest mobile phone that plays to our need for human connection or the branded trainers that we believe will help us feel more liked by others.

We have to remind ourselves of our innate worthiness, our innate goodness, making us the wonderful human beings that we are.

Activity: *Answer these questions*

If you were able to live your life as you desired, what would it look like?

What do you want for yourself but have felt limited by?

If money was no object, what would you want to attract more of in your life?

What do you need to do less of to feel like you are working with purpose and alignment?

What are you ready to embrace in order to give yourself permission to live life as you want?

Who do you need help from?

Now that you are safe, what are you free to create more of in your life?

———

CHAPTER 17

IT'S NOT ABOUT CONTROLLING MONEY

 'I want to be in control of money'.

We've all said words to this effect from time to time. Having control over somebody or something is really a smoke screen for wanting to feel safe. In order to feel safe, we need to accept that money will ebb and flow during our lives, that there will be times of abundance and times of scarcity. And the more we try to control something, the more out of control we become.

Many of us are fearful of change. Change is unfamiliar and the brain dislikes unfamiliarity as it threatens our natural habit patterns. When we think about changing something - our money mindset, our financial situation, our job, something about our business - it feels hard, really difficult. I don't want you to feel that change is hard. I want you to feel that you have the opportunity, the capability, the motivation and desire to step into wealth.

If you are a natural architect around money, you love to plan everything in advance and organise your money because it creates a feeling of safety. And underneath the *behaviour* of planning, the *emotion* is often fear.

What about when our plan doesn't go how we wanted it to? Perhaps we forgot to say something, or the time was not quite right, or we forgot about certain expenses in our spending planner. Again, we feel the fear because we focused on the behaviour and not the emotion sitting behind it. Why do we feel it necessary to have a plan? Often, our behaviours are mirrored from past generations. Did your parents plan everything? Did you observe this growing up?

Everything is about balance. The balance for planning is being more carefree or impulsive (more on this in the *Money Story Types* section). If we can create more spontaneity with our behaviour around money, we can step into that position of certainty where we can recognise it doesn't have to be perfect. It doesn't have to be all mapped out. It doesn't have to be all planned in advance. The minute we're able to feel okay about that, the more possibilities open up.

I have always been really impulsive - with everything! I've always valued this behaviour because I can take risks. I can invest my money in the stock market without feeling fearful about it. I can make quick decisions about my business. I create new ideas every single day (too many sometimes!) but the challenge for me is that because my habits and behaviours are not naturally organised or planned, there can be difficulties like having too many ideas and not being able to focus well on one or two. This can lead to a feeling of overwhelm and chaos, like I am out of control. However, I have learned to trust my natural behaviours and put in place a balance of planning so that it is not over weighted.

This is also about the importance of strong boundaries. Some of you may resonate with this. Some may feel like you make impulsive decisions, perhaps about investing in programmes or memberships or courses that you're buying, or even just purchases in your everyday life. That element of spontaneity can be challenging because it can tip you into debt. Or perhaps you buy something that you don't really need because you're driven by the desire for what you *want*, rather than what you *need*.

Hopefully you can see that it's not so much about creating change as about creating momentum. What is your correct next step into wealth? To feel deserving? To bring money in, holding onto that money and then giving that money out to create the life you want to live?

In order for you to create this momentum, how would it be for you if you just let go of the word *change*? What would happen if you created more trust in yourself and more space for the ebbs and flows of money to come in and out?

Activity: *Answer these questions:*

What do you need to do to create space for money?
What control do you need to let go of?
The opposite of control is ___?
What does that look like?
What do you need to do next to create this for yourself?

Tracey's story: Tracey decided that in order to create space for money she was going to clear out and declutter her wardrobe .... clear space and practise gratitude. Hard core, Marie Kondo style! Within six weeks, she had attracted six high-value clients to her business.

You're getting the theme here, right? Your behaviour is dictated by your beliefs. To change your behaviour you need to change the ways you feel and think. Some of these beliefs are inherited. A lot of our beliefs come from a younger part of ourselves, and our brains will look for evidence to support them, pushing away detail that's too difficult, unfamiliar. The life of debt I lived in my twenties was familiar to me and so I kept attracting more debt. How can we change that behaviour? How can we create a new normal? How can we attract more of what we really seek?

Reluctance to confront our money history - our financial past - comes from a fear of judgement. We worry about judging ourselves. This was huge for me, particularly in my 20s. Underneath the fear of judgement was a lack of self-worth. And underneath that lack of self-worth was a little girl who wanted to be loved and noticed. In the last few years, I've created significant change in the financial industry, and when I say that out loud, I'm uncomfortable. I'm uncomfortable with the attention it can create - I didn't get that attention as a child, and I wanted it ... but I'm not used to it, it feels unfamiliar. As my online visibility grew and people began to talk about my work, I felt uncomfortable. I've had to learn that we naturally seek what we've had a lot of, good or bad, and there comes a time that we need to seek what we didn't have enough of. If you didn't have enough security, freedom, generosity, status, organisation in your younger life, that's what you'll be seeking now.

Carl Jung believed that what remains unconscious does not dissolve but rather resurfaces in our lives as fate or fortune. 'What is not conscious', he said, 'will be experienced as fate'. In other words, we're likely to repeat unconscious patterns of behaviours and beliefs until we bring conscious awareness to them.

Take a moment to think about what repeated patterns you're carrying that do not belong to you?

One of the first money lessons I had was the gift of saving. My dad would empty his pockets of pound coins into a large white ceramic pot each day and we would count them up on the lounge floor, bagging them up into £20 piles and taking them to the bank. Mixed in with the £1 coins were also the other coins - the 20p, 50p and copper coins. I always wanted to be the first to count the £1s, perhaps unconsciously wanting to build a bigger pot than my siblings. The money message here was that it was to be saved, kept safe and every penny accounted for. I remember my dad being so proud of us. It's funny what memories you recall that bring back such happiness.

At the age of around eight, I was walking with my mum to the High Street bank in my local town in Bedfordshire. As she shopped next door, I popped in to update my savings passbook and see how much I had saved. I remember being barely tall enough to peer over the glass screen acting as a barrier between me and the cashier. Even as I type this ... a 'barrier' between the cashier and me? I wonder what message that projected to my unconscious mind at that age? Money was to be guarded? Hidden? Protected? I handed over my passbook and felt excited at the noise of the machine printing black ink into my passbook. The cashier handed it back to me - the balance was a big fat zero. All my money had gone. I daren't ask the cashier what had happened, and I remember an intense feeling of shame and pain. I felt physically sick. Who had taken my money? Where had it gone? Why had I not taken better care of it? Had I done something wrong? I daren't ask my Mum about it because I didn't want her to think I was irresponsible. I never told or asked anybody about it. I simply decided that I was not deserving to receive money and carried that shame into my teenage years.

CHAPTER 18
ARE YOU RUNNING ON AUTO-PILOT?

A re you on *autopilot* in certain areas of your life? Being on autopilot is easy with actions we find comfortable and which we feel more worthy of. You may have a strong beauty routine, yet when it comes to money, it is so unfamiliar that you choose to ignore it. This activity will help you to find out what habits you have on autopilot. Pay some attention to how these habits make you feel.

Activity: *Observe yourself for 48 hours from the perspective of a loving observer.*

Which habits are on autopilot?
How long have you carried out these habits?
Who influenced their creation?
How do these habits serve you?
How do you feel when you don't do them?
What do they tell you about what you value?

CHAPTER 19
OVERSPENDING AND OVERSAVING

Money choices that don't serve you could be due to past trauma. Trauma can cause the brain to overreact. We spend in order to feel safe - on food, alcohol, clothes ... anything that makes us feel good. We're self-medicating the pain away. Overspending can come from needing to be in control. Oversaving can be a way to find safety by hoarding possessions or money. These become cycles of habitual behaviour and, compounded by a lack of planning, can keep us stuck in our financial present state, living for today.

Katrina's story: When I first met Katrina she was in a deep state of not enoughness. She was inconsistent with her saving and spending habits - frugal one minute and blowing her budget the next. She had high-level goals but with no follow-up and she perceived money as a threat. Growing up, treats were rationed, and she was taught never to go into debt. Money was scarce and she attached spontaneity with being irresponsible. She felt afraid to ask for help. Katrina shared with me that when she was made redundant, she felt undeserving of her new job and became terrified at the thought of being made redundant again. She believed that by playing small and not being visible, she could protect herself from the possibility this trauma would repeat itself. She felt terrible about how others had no money and she used possession spending as a way to seek security and comfort. A feeling of more than enoughness did not feel possible for Katrina. Constantly in work mode she fulfilled her need for time freedom by justifying an expensive purchase as a 'need filler'. Together we created a conscious and considered financial plan which helped her to see the consequences of this cycle of overworking and overspending. Her money mantra became: 'I am making conscious and considered decisions'. Katrina eloquently described her emotions around money as *hanging in her wardrobe* and she was beginning to redirect the spending from her wardrobe to her financial future so that she could set a date for when she would no longer have to work. She recognised that her financial values were recognition, freedom, compassion, fairness and integrity and now has a spending plan in alignment, and congruent with, these values.

I shared with Katrina a six-step strategy for identifying some of the root causes of emotional spending:

Ask yourself:

1. Emotion – how did you feel when you spent? Identify what is driving you to make the purchase and challenge the action. Is what you are doing going to make you feel any different in 20 minutes? Remember, your emotional driver could be something really serious. If you are not ready to challenge it then you need to put something in place to prevent you from behaving in that emotional way.
2. Thought – what were you saying to yourself? E.g. 'This pair of jeans will make me feel better'.

3. Behaviour – what did you do as a result of this thought? E.g. grab your phone and start browsing your favourite designer store.
4. Alternative – what could you do instead? Could you leave your phone in another room and do something that feels good, e.g. have a bubble bath or read a book?
5. Motivation – on a scale of 1-10, how motivated do you feel to change?
6. Consequence – what is the consequence of inaction? What will continue to happen if this does not change? Often thinking about the pain of a continued habit can go on to effect change.

Other ways to help you make better decisions as an emotional spender

Evoke a delay

Give yourself 48 hours before purchasing anything. Leaving items in your shopping basket for 48 hours (like a cooling-off period) gives you the space to return to the decision when you are not feeling emotionally triggered. It allows your brain time to think more rationally. You can also choose not to store credit card details online so you have to actually get up and find your purse every time you want to buy something!

Find a new path

Identify what else gives you that emotion. What else could you do that would create the same feeling? A walk in the park? A bubble bath with a glass of your favourite wine? Some time away with friends?

Give yourself freedom

This means permission to treat yourself in other ways, too. Rather than restrict your spending habits entirely, create a separate savings pot, or withdraw some cash and stick it in an envelope. That way, you give yourself permission to spend guilt-free but in alignment with your budget.

Think about your timing

This is important. Don't make big spending decisions during the week. Save them for the weekend when you have more downtime to make better, less emotionally-charged decisions.

Affirm the positive

Make a conscious decision not to use negative language with money. Rather than saying 'I don't have enough money' say something positive like 'I can be in control of my finances.' Look for evidence of the things you are good at. Also, reframe what you are thinking: 'I can be wealthy and increase my income' or 'I can control my spending'. Being conscious about your own money mindset will help you to change your belief systems, leading you to better financial decisions.

What can you do to create the feelings that having a healthy relationship with money gives? Feelings of support, wellbeing, happiness, security and safety ... all of the things we want to be feeling ... and in a time when perhaps you're feeling insecure around money.

CHAPTER 20

OVERWORKING AND UNDEREARNING

U nderearning can also be triggered by trauma. You could be the most highly-educated, talented and capable human being on the planet, yet do not pursue or keep positions for which you are worthy because you feel undeserving.

The symptoms of an underearner are:

- rejecting ideas that could bring more prosperity or profitability to your business;
- finding yourself in a cycle of proving yourself over and over;
- clinging to broken or useless possessions;
- habitually overworking;
- choosing to work alone;
- failing to follow up on opportunities;
- feeling trapped or stuck and showing this in your language

Underearning is a **condition of deprivation** where your emotional or physical needs are not being met. Think about how often you undervalue yourself in your language and how you give your time freely to others. Staying in the habit of underearning will magnify these feelings of unworthiness.

Overworking can arise from feeling that you need to bring in more money in order to be of any value or worth. Ask yourself - are you overworking to:

- be extra articulate (to avoid being misjudged)?
- be extra polite (to avoid retaliation)?
- be extra quiet (to avoid unwanted attention)?
- be extra vigilant (to avoid violence)?
- be extra efficient (to avoid blame)?
- be extra prepared (to avoid undermining)?
- prove yourself (to avoid dismissal and rejection)?

Acknowledging these behaviours and working on your self talk and inherited beliefs can open the gateway for you to begin to heal. Eye Movement Desensitization and Reprocessing (EMDR)[1] and other cognitive therapy can help to heal past traumas. I recently trained in Matrix Reimprinting[2] with Karl Dawson which is incredibly powerful.

CHAPTER 21

WHERE DO OUR BELIEFS COME FROM?

If our relationship with money begins before the age of six, the emotions we attach to money also begin at the start of our lives. Some believe that they go back even further. In dealing with these emotions, we're dealing with the child version of ourselves and the neural pathways through which they've been created. To create new neural pathways we have to bring these emotions to the fore, see those patterns of behaviour, of belief ... the stories and the meaning we attach to those stories.

During my 20s I yearned for money to buy more clothes and feel better in myself. If I felt better in myself, more people would notice me and like me. That belief had been in me for many years. As a child at primary school, I created a beautiful piece of work one day. My handwriting was perfect, but I made an error and screwed up the paper and threw it to the ground. I ran to the toilets, crying, and stood on top of the toilet seat in the cubicle so nobody would see my feet. Nobody came.

What that taught me was that unless I was perfect, nobody cared. Nobody knew I was there. I was not important enough to be noticed, and if nobody was noticing me, I didn't matter. Many of you will have had similar experiences, underpinning the belief that you are not worthy of money or, conversely, *rich people are greedy*. This is because our beliefs are embedded, imprinted on our minds and sit in our memory bank. They underpin our conversations about money. All of those influences - societal, cultural, religious, family - create a blueprint, a pattern that travels down through the generations.

How we feel and behave with money is driven by so many things: external factors like social media, family pressures/influence, friendship/peer groups; our internal influences - our personalities and belief systems, personal experiences both conscious and unconscious. We see Instagram images of this perfect world with women lying in baths and rose petals scattered everywhere ... a glass of wine, candles lit and not a rubber duck or lego brick (or is that just me!) in sight. We also form judgements. You might see one of those pictures and think 'She's so vain' or 'It would be delightful to have a beautiful bath like that'. Those judgments are not new. They have formed because of what already exists within our unconscious beliefs around money. Additionally, the way the media speaks to us as women about money sends a message that having wealth is either bad, greedy and mean or that you're a rich girl and you haven't earned it. There are very few films I can think of that depict strong women with money who are actually nice. The only one that comes to mind is Disney's *Frozen 2* (yes - I know they are princesses).

Growing up, fairy tales were a major part of my childhood. So many of the films depicted women as 'weak' females in some type of distress who not only needed a man to rescue her, but whose biggest focus was on romantic love and the quest to marry Prince Charming. These stereotypes did not provide for strong female role models of independence and resilience. *Frozen 2*, however, includes two strong, independent female protagonists, and shifts the focus away from romantic love towards family and self-love.

What impact did the films you were exposed to growing up have on your unconscious beliefs? How have they stopped you from making progress?

As women we often feel uncomfortable selling our products, even when we know they're excellent. How many of you have thought your products are so excellent you're going to give them away for free? Or: *I think this is a really good product, but if I just maybe change the colour a little bit, then I'll be confident enough to sell it.* Or: *If I just build my website first, then maybe I'll feel confident enough to sell it.* Or: *If I just lose 10 pounds, then I'll be able to sell it.* We look for justification for not selling our thing! This is why it's so important to focus on yourself.

I see opportunity in everything - every lesson, every painful experience, every pleasurable experience, *everything* has opportunity. Every day that we wake up, every experience, every lesson we have is an opportunity.

CHAPTER 22
PARENTS

By now, you may be wondering how much of your relationship with money has come from your parents. By far the biggest influence on how we feel about money comes from who has brought us up - parents, grandparents, guardians.

What is your earliest experience of money? If you grew up with little, did that lead you to a scarcity mindset in which you had to hoard it? Or did you go in the opposite direction and feel like every time you earned money you wanted to spend it?

A client of mine told me about his mum. She never talked about money but would always leave her credit card statements on the side. He would look at them and wonder why, when she was paying against them every month, the capital never came down. It got him thinking about interest and led to a fear of the position his mum was in.

Tracing back your family's historical beliefs around money could reveal a lot about your own anxieties, fears and beliefs. It could also help you to ask some potent questions of yourself and family members. What messages did you hear around money growing up? Who was responsible for money in the house? Did your family have money? Or never enough? Create some multi-generational patterns.

Ask these questions of your parents and - if you are able - your grandparents, as well as brothers and sisters or family members that were around when you were younger. What multi-generational patterns begin to appear?

Money beliefs that have come from our parents and parents' parents are resistant to change. What your six-year-old self believed about herself sits in your unconscious mind even as an adult. What would that six-year-old need to hear in order to feel self-worth? What is she resisting? Maybe she heard some negative messages around money, about how you should work hard for it. Some of you may have grown up with strong religious backgrounds, another influence that can filter through generationally. I've heard some fascinating stories from women who have multi-generational stories of control of money through scarcity. Despite cultural changes, the belief still exists. My grandfather was in a Japanese prisoner of war camp and there was a lot of scarcity in the UK when he came out weighing around five and a half stone. His favourite food before he went into the camp was rice pudding so his Mum, my Great Grandmother, made him a beautiful rice pudding dish. He couldn't eat it because all he'd lived on for years was rice. His relationship with food was created by his experience. Has my relationship with food been passed down the generations so that I'm not allowed to feel good about it? Even without our parents speaking about it overtly, have we taken on their beliefs simply by being in their environment?

Leaving our inherited beliefs unchallenged can render them ours, and then our children's beliefs. In challenging them we should question if they're even real - or just a *belief*. A belief is not necessarily true, right? If you're operating from your parents' beliefs, are these actually true? Or just beliefs?

Activity: *Healing other people's money narratives*

Draw five columns on a sheet of paper:

Column 1 - My parents'/main caregivers' money narratives and
stories
Column 2 - The Meaning
Column 3 - The Emotion
Column 4 - Truth or Perception?
Column 5 - New Belief

MY MAIN CAREGIVER'S MONEY NARRATIVE	THE MEANING	THE EMOTION	TRUTH OR PERCEPTION?	NEW BELIEF

For example, Mum's belief - *food treats are limited to Sundays*.
The meaning I attached to that was: *food is limited therefore
there is never enough*.
The emotion here is: *fear and scarcity*.
Truth or perception? *Perception* (It is not true!)
The new belief to counterbalance this is: *There is more than
enough*.
What conclusions can you draw from this?
What links can you acknowledge? Are these beliefs actually
true?

CHAPTER 23
CARRIED EMOTIONS

Many of the beliefs we carry are borrowed. I want you to imagine that you have a giant sack flung over your shoulder like Father Christmas, and inside this sack are gifts beautifully wrapped up. Inside each one of those gifts is a piece of paper hidden inside, like a fortune cookie. Each of these messages is a borrowed belief and attached to this belief is a borrowed emotion. Many of these beliefs are not true (like Father Christmas!) but rather stories that have been passed down the generations - from grandmother to mother, from mother to daughter, from daughter to grandchildren. These beliefs are based upon our memories, some of which are small and some of which are big. Many of the beliefs and carried emotions inside this sack serve us well, helping us to make positive decisions with money ... but some of them sabotage our lives. These are the ones we should give back, with love, to whoever gave them to us so that they are not carried into future generations. Memories of childhood experiences should be unwrapped and rewrapped, this time in new, bright, shiny wrapping paper. Paper that sparkles. Paper that creates joy and happiness. A new positive belief.

Each little belief inside that sack has an emotion. The emotions we attach to these beliefs are *carried* emotions. They have been given to us. We have inherited or learned them from parents, caregivers and important adults in our society and culture. Carried emotions lead us to react to the situation happening to us now as if it were someone else's situation in the past, as if we are carrying the same emotional sequence of someone else's past into our current reality. By virtue of carrying other people's emotions with us, we lose access to our own authentic emotions, our own feelings, or our own thoughts about a situation. This can lead to a lack of clarity about our own identity or ability to make our own unbiased decisions. And we lose that internal intuition that kicks in to tell us what feels right for us. We continue to drag this belief bag from our own shoulders and pass this onto future generations.

Think about a belief that you inherited from your parents or main caregiver:

Investing is only for those who are wealthy.

Rich people are greedy.

Pensions are bad. You can lose them.

You'll never be successful as an artist.

Never spend more than you earn.

Unconsciously, we attempt to rid ourselves of these 'carried' emotions by blaming others so that we can feel that temporary release of incompetence we carry. But soon we're back - feeling stupid, worthless, shameful, not good enough, unlovable, incapable, irresponsible or superior.

For many years I carried a huge amount of shame about having money. I associated having money with being greedy and worthy and my own deep sense of unworthiness wanted to get rid of it as quickly as I made it. I would come up with an internal excuse to justify it: 'I just really needed some new make-up because the seven eyeliners I already have aren't very good'; or 'I won't charge *that* much for my service because I want to help as many people as possible.'

I was paralysing myself. I was addicted to the struggle. I was addicted to focusing on my outgoings, to what was flowing out of my account faster than I could blink!

Whose shame are you carrying?

Wow. It isn't always our own narratives about money that we carry. We can operate from scarcity or *lack of* from generations of women in our families who were not wealthy, women whose wealth was given to someone else, women whose wealth was lost through businesses that didn't succeed, women whose wealth was controlled by their partners, women whose wealth was passed on to the men.

Society also *'shoulds'* on us to focus on our expenses, to limit our spending and to manage our budgets. I started focusing on my income instead. I was more comfortable making more money, and by releasing the shame I was carrying, and being able to *hold onto* more wealth, I changed my entire life. It wasn't just money that I was carrying shame around either! It was like this sudden connection with money helped me unlock other areas in which I felt unfulfilled. It literally unlocked everything.

We all inhabit generational belief patterns ... an *inter-generational wealth belief*. Now, right now, I want you to create a healthy financial legacy for yourself and every single possible future generation.

Do you argue with your partner about money and feel like you're coming at it from totally different perspectives? Money isn't the problem. We know that now. Our reactions stem from unresolved beliefs from our past. Perhaps that belief is triggering us into deprivation mode. And then we calm down and look at the figures and think: 'Oh ... actually it's fine. We can deal with this'. We each have beliefs about money that we can't speak out loud and this avoidance creates biases. It can mean we avoid doing certain things or making certain choices and can remain unchallenged for years (more on how to handle these conversations in the Create section).

It goes without saying that you want your children to have
everything that you didn't have ... and you want your children to
have things that you *did* have. There is nothing wrong with either of
those. But one of the biggest challenges is self-sabotage ... and you
now need to let go of any borrowed beliefs that are not serving you.

Activity: On a *piece of paper draw four columns with these
headings:*

*Borrowed Beliefs, Who, Benefits, Challenges. Under the first heading
write some of the borrowed beliefs you have inherited. Who gave
them to you? What are the benefits of holding onto these beliefs? What
are the challenges if you continue to hold onto them?*

BORROWED BELIEFS	WHO?	BENEFITS	CHALLENGES

These areas are very resistant to change, but the likelihood is
that if you had that belief, somebody else has also had that
belief. There's something really powerful about being
vulnerable and opening up about this.

How far back could you trace these beliefs in your family? Is it time for you to give these back (with love of course)? Hold on to the elements that will support you and give back the ones that won't.

I received a message from Judith in April 2021 which touched my heart.

Judith's story: *I enjoy your podcast and your Instagram posts, some of which say we should tell you what we think. So I will!*

I was introduced to you from a tiny quote on Gemma Cairney's[1] Instagram feed on 10th April (my birthday!) this year after you had both taken part in an event with Stylist Magazine. I didn't see the event, I just saw Gemma's post afterwards. She had collected some nuggets of wisdom, one of which was you saying that it is 'important to look at whose shame we're carrying'. Those words have changed my life. Even typing them out now after I've worked with them for several weeks, I'm getting emotional.

I'm out of debt. I mean, I've got the same amount of debt I had when I read your words, but I'm organised. I've closed two of my three credit cards and am making the remaining one work for me. I'm finally saving, both in a Lifetime ISA and in a separate account to cover my Open University costs ahead of time rather than panicking that I won't be able to afford the next module of my engineering degree. I've been able to identify the emotional reasons for my actions with money and spot where I've been living what I was shown growing up.

My mother has a desperate need to be loved so has spent her life in acts of service to people who not only didn't ask for them but are generally not in the least bit grateful when they're complete. I have been mirroring this. Your guidance has helped me realise that not only have I been devoting my money to other people but I've been doing the same with my time and my energy. I have consciously turned MY resources inwards for MY own benefit, which

I'd heard about but wasn't in the right place to do anything with before. It felt selfish but I realise now that it isn't the case at all.

Your words on Gemma Cairney's Instagram were the stone that started the avalanche for me and I will be forever grateful.

Thank you.

Your story is just that – a *story*. In order for it to serve you, you must rewrite it, and to do that you must accept where you are right now with integrity and honesty.

Activity: *Dear Money*

Imagine money as a friend.
What would you be saying to it right now?
'Money, we've had a difficult relationship this year.'
'Money, I don't trust you.'
'Money, I feel motivated by you.'
Write a letter to Money.
Tell it how you feel about it right now.

Here is an extract from when I wrote to *Money* in 2000:

Dear Money

I found you today, all crumpled up in the bottom of another unused handbag. I am sorry I have mistreated you so much, but I am struggling to understand you.

Sometimes I spend you and you make me feel so good. Sometimes for an hour, sometimes for weeks on end. But sometimes I spend you and then I feel guilty. Shameful. What happens if I don't have you anymore? I receive you with ease yet I get rid of you quicker than I can type.

I was taught to have more of you to help others. That you are to be used to control others. That you are to be kept hidden away.

You are to be loved.

To be taken care of but also given some freedom.

I appreciate you most when I remember that you are nothing to do with me. My sense of self.

Having more of you does not mean I am worthy of more.

Having more of you does not mean that more people will like me.

Having more of you will not make me feel more fulfilled.

Having more of you will not make me feel more loved.

I am capable of giving myself love, as the adult. I am able to give the six-year-old version of myself a cuddle and tell her that she is safe, and she is loved.

In fact, you are really just a coin with two sides.

One side an opportunity for me to give and the other for me to receive.

I honour both in equal measure and I am ready to treat you with respect.

To keep you out of the closet.

I am ready to acknowledge that you have no emotion.

You are just a coin.

I am just me.

Little old me.

I am safe.

I am loved.

I am enough.

Changing beliefs doesn't happen overnight. If that belief is: *I can't charge X amount for this service ... I'm not deserving enough because my dad told me this and my mum said that*, or *I can't charge X amount for this service because I was bullied at school, and I had lack of self-worth* - what would it feel like for you to release that? What would it feel like for you to say: *I am comfortable to charge X for my service, and that would enable me to double my impact in the world?* What would that actually feel like? Would it feel empowering? Successful? Deserving?

CHAPTER 24
GAINS

J ust as you have now released some inherited beliefs, take a moment to think about what your beliefs help you to avoid, ways that you are benefiting from your story. This is called *secondary gain*.

Activity: *Find the secondary gain*

Write this on a piece of paper: *What am I gaining by holding on to those beliefs?*
And then: *What are the challenges of having that belief?*
Example belief: *Money doesn't grow on trees*

CURRENT BELIEF: _____

WHAT ARE YOU GAINING?	THE CHALLENGE	FLIP THE COIN	HOW MOTIVATED?	HOW WILLING?	WHO DO YOU NEED TO HELP?

1) *What are you gaining from having that belief?*
Acceptance of this belief might mean you can avoid talking about money and pass on money responsibilities (and the emotions attached to them) to someone else. Perhaps an advantage is that you're a hard worker - great when there's a challenge or a job that needs to be done.

2) *What is the challenge for you of having that belief?*
A challenge might be that you feel you have to work 14 hours a day in order to be successful, thereby not seeing much of your family/friends, being constantly exhausted and suffering with your mental health. But if you work 70 hours a week because you fear there'll never be enough money - guess what? That belief will become the foundation of how you make your money decisions.

3) *Flip the coin - what would happen if you did or felt the complete opposite of that belief? What would be possible?*
What needs to happen right now for you to make that happen? What is one thing you can do straight away?

4) *How motivated are you to make this change?*

5) *How willing are you to make this change?*

6) *Who do you need to help you to make this change?*

Begin this journey of creating new habits with a simple step. Don't overwhelm yourself - think about one thing at a time that you could do differently in order to build resilience, challenge the thoughts and emotions and change the behaviour. It is all about creating momentum. Small steps, big wins.

CHAPTER 25

YOUR FINANCIAL BLUEPRINT

B e honest with yourself about this - do you have an *abundance
mindset* or a *scarcity mindset*? Do you think more about financial
struggle or about an abundance of money? We're all born with a
financial blueprint and the emotions we carry around about money
have been there a long time. Your relationship with money has been
created by memories and experiences prior to the age of six.

I'm going to get a little *science and geeky* with you here!

The dominant brainwave of conscious adults is called *Beta*, which
creates a state of mind characterised as *active or focused consciousness*.
This is the state of fully conscious mental activity for most adults,
most of the time they are awake. The dominant brainwave pattern of
children two years old and younger is *Delta*. This is the slowest
brainwave pattern and is dominant during deep sleep for children of
all ages, and also adults.

Delta waves create a state of mind that is open and receptive to
influences, as opposed to being logical, rational and less open to new
ideas. During this brainwave and its consequential state of mind,
children are learning and absorbing ideas and beliefs from adults all

around them, as well as taking in vast amounts of new information from their senses.

After the age of three, memories are recorded and processed by the hippocampus, a part of the limbic system of the brain that processes new memories for long-term storage.

The dominant brainwave of children between two and five years of age is in the *Theta* range. This brainwave creates a state of mind that is relaxed and calm in adults. During this brainwave and its consequential state, the mind is open and receptive to ideas and beliefs and the influence of others. This is a critical period of mental and psychological development where children are adopting the ideas and beliefs of their parents and other significant caregivers.

'Young children carefully observe their environment and download the worldly wisdom offered by their parents, directly into the subconscious memory. As a result, their parent's behavior and beliefs become their own.' Dr. Bruce Lipton from *The Biology of Belief*[1].

Ok - so I am done with the science lesson, but how incredible is that! For those of you with children, I bet right now you are thinking about what you might say to them today!

So, if those messages were messages of scarcity - *you have to work hard; look after the pennies and the pounds will look after themselves* - they would have passed on to you and sat in your unconscious belief system. We all have these core money scripts, so deeply ingrained in our belief systems that unless we take the time to examine them consciously, recognise them and consider the power they have, we won't know they exist. And they are all centered around emotion. Here are a few examples of money stories we typically hold:

I need to be in control of money.

I need to start believing in myself.

I want to grow my business.

I should be getting out there.

I'm happy to be financially dependent.

I hate being financially dependent.

I hoard money ... I must not spend it.

People who hoard money are tight.

You may know somebody who quibbles over £2.00 on a restaurant bill. You think they're 'tight'. Consider another possibility - that something happened in their childhood that taught them that being frivolous with money is good. Perhaps the messages they heard suggested this.

Unconscious beliefs affect our decisions which, in turn, lead to our actions or inactions. Many of us focus on creating more money consciously and yet, at an unconscious level, have blocks or limiting beliefs holding us back. We need to bring those beliefs to the surface and unravel them.

Activity: *Identify your core belief about money*

Does any of this sound familiar?
I don't deserve to have money.
I shouldn't earn more money than my spouse.
People who have money are bad and people who are poor are good.
Money is evil.
Money destroys worthwhile relationships.
I shouldn't spend money on myself. It's really selfish/extravagant.
If I have lots of money, I'll just be like those other rich people that I really don't like.
You have to choose between love and money. You can't have both.
I have to work myself to pure exhaustion to make more money.
Asking for money is greedy.

What are you gaining from holding on to that belief? What would happen if you weren't to believe it, do the opposite, focus on creating a new belief? What would happen if you thought: *money comes easily and freely and I am able and I am worthy to attract wealth?*

Activity: *Complete this statement:* Money is ...

Do it quickly without thinking too hard. What comes up? What does money mean to you? Power? Fame? Happiness? Status? Abundance? Or is it hard work? Scarcity?

The second statement I want you to complete is: *Money feels ...*
What emotion comes up for you? You can add it on to the first sentence if you like, e.g. *Money is scarce and it feels scary. Money is scarce and it feels anxious. Money is happiness and it feels good. Money is challenging and it feels unclear.*

The third sentence to complete is: *In my family money meant ...* This could be a couple of sentences or even a paragraph.

The final sentence to complete is: *I feel ... about my finances ...* Be honest. Get right under the bonnet of those emotions. The reason I'm getting you to do this now is that I want you to very gently tip up some of the emotions that are going on for you.

We all want to have enough money and be financially secure, and this means different things to different people. What does 'enough' mean to you? Are you in a space of *enoughness*? Are you in a space of *not enoughness?* Or are you in a space of *more than enoughness?* We all want to get into a position of awareness around our finances. Having awareness gives us choice, security. In reality, lack of money fuels fear, negative beliefs and negative patterns. To break those patterns, we need to do two things: reaffirm the positive things about money and begin to think differently. How many of you feel you have to hold on to money? Perhaps you have a fear of spending. Did you hear the message: *don't spend what you haven't earned?* And when you do spend, do you feel guilty?

The thing is, the minute we get out of our own way, oh my gosh - the world will open up to so many opportunities. And the thing that will get us out of our own way is *change*. We may not like change, but it gives us an opportunity to build those financial resiliency muscles.

A typical behavioural cycle is to overspend, pay all that debt off - insisting it won't happen again - and being back there six months later. The problem here is the attempt to change the *behaviour*, when it's the thought process behind the behaviour that needs to change. *Change the thought to change the emotion to change the behavior.* In *Atomic Habits*[2], James Clear explains how you have to prepare your mind to change the action before you actually believe it's possible that you're motivated. This, in turn, attaches a positive emotion to that new behaviour. So - if you're filled with dread every time you think of going to the gym, you're not likely to go ... it sits outside your comfort zone. And nobody likes doing anything outside their comfort zone. If it fills you with positivity, you'll do it.

I am not a big believer in personality profiling, especially when it comes to money. In fact, we should always be aware of the language we use around money. If we tell ourselves that we are overgivers, our brain will seek evidence to support that belief. At the same time, having awareness of our money behaviours will help us to choose the most effective practical steps for moving forwards and achieving more balance with those habits. To move into a position of greater flow and greater acceptance of our natural habits and the ones that we need to call upon.

To this end, we have created five *Money Story Types*™ to help you examine your own style and motivations on this journey to a more positive and fulfilling relationship with money. I do not want you, however, to use the outcomes of these story types as a label. You are not money!

Activity: *Identify your Money Story Types*™

Head over to www.itsnotaboutthemoney.com/quiz
You can also do this on paper. Put a tick in the box next to the *Money Story Types*™ that you align with most right now. You may find you align to more than one - that's OK. If so, think about which one is your primary and which is your secondary narrative. Add a number 1 and number 2 next to the ones you associate with the most.

◻ The Impulsive StoryType

Current Narrative: '*I am out of control with money*'

New Narrative: '*It is safe for me to save and spend*'

Your primary beliefs: Your brain believes that you have to spend money to be accepted by others. You don't feel good enough, and therefore don't feel like you ever have enough. When money comes to you, you often find yourself feeling that it must be spent. In fact, the belief is so strong that perhaps you spend money before it even reaches you. Your conscious mind tells you that you are powerless to control your spending.

Your supportive money narrative: You are an action taker. You are super-reactive to opportunities and can make swift decisions, which can be both a blessing and a challenge. In your life, you truly value enjoyment, both your own and others. Others love to be around you - your energy is intoxicating. Short bursts of adrenaline make you feel alive.

Your sabotaging money narrative: The brain has learned that these adrenaline shots can be achieved by continuing the impulsive narratives it believes to be true and you may consequently find it hard to sit still. What most people don't know is that when you're alone you worry about your lack of focus. You crave a little structure, and above all, a feeling of safety. Your brain doesn't want to give up its adrenaline shots, and so your efforts to add structure to your life have felt restrictive and boring, and therefore short-lived. You long for a life which combines your zest for life and adventure with the craving you have for security and safety.

Your balancing money narrative:

The *Money Story Types*™ that will best support you to achieve some balance between the supportive and the sabotaging money story type is **The Architect StoryType.**

☐ The Enabler StoryType

Current Narrative: 'I am safer to give than to receive'

New Narrative: 'It is safe for me to spend money on myself with no guilt'

Your primary beliefs: Your brain believes that helping others is the biggest marker of being a good person. In fact, the brain has so much evidence for this belief that it has concluded that people who want to spend money on themselves are frivolous, selfish or materialistic. In your drive to leave a legacy of being a good person, you have rejected all behaviours which the brain believes will make you a bad person.

Your supportive money narrative: You are an excellent and diligent caretaker of others, an adept problem solver and are generous with both your time and money. You value investing your money in ways that can support the environment and causes that align with your values.

Your sabotaging money narrative: You reject opportunities to take care of yourself. Receiving gifts is difficult for you, and even harder is spending money on yourself. It is easy to slip into over-enabling, something that restricts others' ability to develop their own balanced *Money Narrative*. You don't often place enough value on your own time and time for yourself and can feel resentful when you spend money on others and this is not appreciated.

Your balancing money narrative: The *Money StoryTypes*™ that will best support you to achieve some balance between the supportive and the sabotaging money story type is **The Innovator or The Architect StoryType.**

The Architect StoryType

Current Narrative: 'I am not safe to spend money that is unplanned'

New Narrative: 'It is safe for me to be impulsive and feel secure'

Your primary beliefs: Your brain believes that money is limited. There will never be enough. If money is limited, the resulting behaviour is to plan for every eventuality. In fact, you have honed your planning skills to near perfection!

Your supportive money narrative: You are an excellent project manager who plans and manages like a boss. The brain has collected evidence to support the belief that those who work the hardest get the most money which means that you have a strong work ethic.

Your narrative means that you're not the type of person to be tempted by 'get rich quick' schemes and are least likely to fall into investment traps.

Your sabotaging money narrative: Issues may arise when you need to step into implementation. This can mean that you often struggle to take the necessary action linked to your plan, and this leads to feelings of frustration. Deviating from the plan reinforces the belief that there is never enough money. You need to be mindful of your boundaries so as to be careful not to burn out. You can be blind to the opportunities around you which means you may miss out on making financial decisions that support you.

Your balancing money narrative: The *Money Story Types*™ that will best support you to achieve some balance between the supportive and the sabotaging money story type is **The Impulsive StoryType.**

☐ The Pacifist StoryType

Current Narrative: 'I am not worried about money as something will come up, it always does.'

New Narrative: 'It is safe for me to take responsibility with money'

Your primary beliefs: Your brain believes that money is something to avoid at all costs. As a result of this, you avoid money. The belief is that money is a necessary evil. In order to avoid conflict, you pay as little attention to money as possible. You are not driven by material goods or possessions, but instead by your passion for living life, connecting with others, and enjoying each moment.

Your supportive money narrative: You are a passionate humanitarian. Your brain believes that it must avoid conflict and suffering at all costs and knowing that others are in such dire need upsets you deeply. You want to leave this world better than you found it. You are creative at seeking ways to do this, often through means other than money. You often find creative ways to enjoy life.

Your sabotaging money narrative: You believe that money is the root of all conflict and suffering and as a result you avoid money. You see money as a necessary evil. You often pay as little attention to money as possible. You might say 'Money just isn't important to me'. You can very quickly slip into immaturity or irresponsibility with money.

Your balancing money narrative: The *Money Story Types*™ that will best support you to achieve some balance between the supportive and the sabotaging money story type is **The Architect or The Innovator StoryType.**

☐ The Innovator StoryType

Current Narrative: 'I am a money maker. I can just create more of it.'

New Narrative: 'It is safe for me to enjoy today and look to the future.'

Your primary beliefs: Your brain believes that money is a tool you can use to realise your plans for financial independence. In fact, your brain is so focused on its future self that it often forgets to take care of the present self. The brain is robbing from Peter to give to Paul. There is a belief, perhaps unconscious, that you are far better than others with money. Money works for you, it is abundant and all around you, and this belief makes you feel superior.

Your supportive money narrative: You are comfortable to take risks and see opportunities all around you. Your brain is so focused on the future self result that you work tirelessly in pursuit of the goal. You have a strong work ethic. You are an adept decision-maker and make decisions swiftly and confidently. When a decision you make doesn't pay off, you accept the lesson and move on.

Your sabotaging money narrative: You can slip into excessive risk-taking or say yes to too many things. You need to be careful that you take care of the present self and don't slip into burnout.

Your balancing money narrative: The *Money StoryTypes™* that will best support you to achieve some balance between the supportive and the sabotaging money story type is **The Pacifist StoryType.**

CHAPTER 27
MONEY NARRATIVES CLEARING®

Now that you have identified your primary and secondary narratives, the next step, *Money Narratives Clearing®*, is the process of examining your current Narrative, accepting it and thanking it for the ways in which it has supported you, understanding (without judgement) the ways in which this sabotages your behaviours and using these insights to rewrite and give a different meaning and perception to these money narratives.

Are you ready? Now is your time to be that wealthy woman.

This often means examining, clearing and redefining the meaning of these beliefs. The meaning that we attach to our experiences and events is what creates the emotions that sit behind that. This, in turn, creates the behaviours based on what the brain now believes to be fact and fiction.

Money Narratives Clearing® is the process of finding balance between the five predominant money stories. As a reminder, these are:

The Impulsive StoryType

The Enabler Storytype

The Architect StoryType

The Pacifist StoryType

The Innovator StoryType

There is no right or wrong Narrative with money or in life. There are no good or bad stories. There are just stories. Each story presents its own unique challenges and advantages. We call these **sabotaging** and **supporting**. *The key to Money Narratives Clearing® is rewriting your most dominant Narrative in order to tell your brain a more balanced story.*

Activity: *The Three Questions of Release, Possibility and Meaning*

Work through these three powerful questions:

1. What is it now time for you to let go of?
2. What will be possible now?
3. What would this mean to your life?

RELEASE: It is time for me to let go of the feeling of (insert the feeling) and embrace the new narrative that money is (enter what you want to be saying about money).

POSSIBILITY: This new narrative will help me to (enter the possibilities)

MEANING: What these possibilities will mean for me are (enter what it means for you)

CHAPTER 28

YOUR FINANCIAL COMFORT ZONE

Money is about receiving, retaining and giving

We all have a specific amount of money in mind that makes us feel comfortable, safe, financially secure. But this zone can also keep us stuck in unhealthy patterns and prevent us from receiving more, retaining more and giving more.

Think about your bank account. At what point do you feel uneasy? When your balance gets down to £50? When it gets to £500? £1000? £5000? Or is it when you're in your overdraft? Where's your safety level? At which point do you feel not worthy of that wealth? At which point do you tip out of your financial comfort zone and feel fear, guilt, shame or judgement?

We've all witnessed people with nothing winning the lottery and becoming millionaires, only to have spent it all within a few years. Sudden windfalls can push us outside our boundaries. Many lottery winners have gone bankrupt because they don't know how to deal with it.

I know people who hold on to their comfort level in one account by shimmying anything above it into another account, thereby not seeing it and avoiding those emotions. When I was in my twenties and living in my overdraft each month, my zone was most comfortable when my balance was at minus £2,000. When my account showed a positive balance, it was so unfamiliar to me that I felt undeserving and uncomfortable. It sounds odd to say, but a negative balance became the limit of my comfort zone. And it was limiting *me*. In the *Create* section of this book, I share with you the importance of your relationship with savings habits as well as debt patterns for this very reason. As soon as I began to build my savings balance, I became more motivated to save more and pay more of my debts off as my comfort zone stretched.

How can *you* stretch that comfort zone? How can you normalise wealth?

I'm a big believer in helping you break through some of those comfort levels. It is only beyond the comfort zone that greater possibilities exist, not just by having more money, but in feeling better with it.

I'm now going to guide you through an exercise that will help you focus on the light and the dark ... the possibilities and the fears. Fears fuel money pain so understanding them can help to feel the pain *and* release it. We should not be afraid to feel emotion. Emotions need to flow.

Activity: *Find your financial comfort zone.*

Start with a little bit of money, let's say £100.
Write down how you feel about receiving this £100.

Light - *What is possible for you now that you have this?*
Dark - *What do you think will happen now that you have received this?*

Let's expand this ... what happens when you have a little bit more money?

If I give you another £100, you have £200, so finish this sentence for me: *Having more money means ...*

How about if I gave you £1000? How does this feel?

What impact would it have on you and on your relationships?

What impact would this have on your time?

How about £100,000? £250,000? £500,000?

What about £1,000,000? £5,000,000?

Have you identified a financial comfort level here?

These comfort zones are artificial financial boundaries that we impose on ourselves. Choosing to live at the end of your financial comfort zone so you can invest for the future is one of the most important ways to build long term financial independence and lasting financial comfort.

What does that tell you about yourself? What kind of emotions is this bringing out for you right now?
How can you receive money in a way that talks more to the light than to the dark side? How can you gently stretch that comfort zone?

From that exercise you may have established that you felt quite comfortable with £100, but perhaps a little bit uncomfortable with £1000. Maybe you identified that this £1000 reminded you of a time when receiving felt excessive or wrong. A gift at Christmas time, perhaps? Now ask yourself *who?* Who gave you this belief?

I experienced a huge shift around this for myself in 2020. My business had the best year, financially, that I had ever experienced, even from working at the bank many years ago when I was on a high salary. 2020 was the year I broke the ceiling and ... it didn't feel good ... it didn't feel bad ... it just was what it was. I was always used to just getting rid of money and here I was receiving more than I'd ever had before. And then, finally, all of that transformational work I'd done with myself over the years won through and I felt worthy. It gave me confidence and increased self-belief. It meant I could create more impact in the world - something that meant more than any bank balance net worth figure could ever have. Has my life changed because I'm wealthier? No. I'm still who I am. However, it's enabled me to create more impact and value in the world, and that's what I do.

I no longer have a problem stating how much I charge for my services. I offer different levels of service so it's easier for me to say to someone who balks at the cost that if they can't afford to come into my course, they have access to my podcast. Alternatively, I can offer them a free download or suggest they read this book. I have worked my business in a way that enables me to engage with as many women as I can but also to have the financial success, I need to create the impact I want to have in the world.

Where does that sit with you in terms of your job, your profession, your career, your business? Where is your comfort level?

Meaningful change doesn't have to be radical. You don't have to make huge decisions about your finances. A change is meaningful if it means something to you, and sometimes that involves *unlearning* as much as learning. Unlearning is much harder to do but it can all begin with a simple awareness of your language.

Imagine receiving just 10% more money than you do now. Many of us would feel comfortable with receiving or asking for a small amount. The larger increases are problematic because our nervous system feels they are unfamiliar and unsafe. Remember that this all stems from the conditioned beliefs we developed during childhood manifesting into our financial present. When we find ourselves outside of what we are comfortable with we don't feel like we belong.

How do you stretch this comfort zone?

1. Make it a conscious decision to expand your comfort zone by small incremental amounts.
2. Learn how to manage and make money (more on that in the *Create* section).
3. Learn to be more comfortable with more, and with less.
4. Avoid the trap of thinking that you have to make radical change. Great change doesn't mean radical change. Small steps, big wins!

Now that you are astute in your relationship with money, you are ready to step into Step Two - *Create*. This is where you will get practical with money. Look at you! Already becoming that wealthy woman!

Small steps. Big wins. Let's go!

'Don't buy the things you can't afford, with money that you don't have, to impress the people that you don't actually like.'

— **DAVE RAMSEY**

CHAPTER 29
CREATING WEALTH AND PROSPERITY

Get ready to move from your financial past into your financial present.

Moving from your *past* to your *present* in how you feel and behave with money may take some time. Change work is also not linear so even when we do the deep work on our relationship with money to prepare ourselves to feel deserving of having wealth, wealth creation is not linear. Like any relationship, it takes nurturing, love, attention and growth.

When I think about creating wealth, what I am super curious about is what does it actually mean? When we seek financial freedom, what are we really seeking? I often sit in a hot bubble bath for hours on end pondering over the meaning of life and my place within it. There is one thing that I am certain of: creating wealth is not just about creating more money.

It's not about the money.

If we refer to etymology for a moment, the expression *to create* means *to bring into existence* and it comes from the Middle English: *createn, borrowed from Latin creātus, past participle of creāre - to bring into being, beget, give birth to, cause to grow.*

So, what is it that we want to bring into being? To give birth to? To grow? I want to open your mind to what you wish to create ... More wealth? Prosperity? Abundance? Does it actually matter? Let's explore where these words come from and what they mean.

Wealth - in economics the word *wealth* is defined as *the accumulation of resources - physical assets, e.g. your home and savings, minus liabilities, e.g your mortgage.* The problem with this definition is the suggestion that in order to be wealthier we have to have more *assets.* Yet we know that *more* doesn't necessarily equal greater happiness!

In etymology, *wealth* comes from the old English *weal,* which means 'wealth, welfare, and wellbeing'. *Weal* is, in turn, related to the older word *wel,* meaning 'in a state of good fortune, welfare, or happiness'.

Wel gives birth to *welth* around 1250 AD, and *welthi* a century or so later. By 1430 it seems to have settled around the idea of riches and prosperity, leaving behind the older meanings of wider wellbeing and health.

So what we are saying here is that we have nearly 600 years of language to contend with. Not easy when, as a woman, we are already contending with gender inequality.

Prosperity - This comes from the Latin *prosperitatem* (nominative *prosperitas*) meaning 'good fortune', and directly from the word *prosperus* -

flourishing or thriving condition, good fortune, wealth, success in anything good or desirable.

While *prosperity* and *wealth* are often used interchangeably, *prosperity* creates the feeling of more expansiveness. Prosperity is the state of *being* wealthy, or having a rich and full life.

Abundance is more about contentment - From Old French *abondance* and directly from the Latin *abundantia* -'fullness, plenty', *abundance* is a feeling of plenty, with the peace of mind that there's enough. When we are in a mindset of abundance, the sense of limitedness is removed, leading to less competition, less of a feeling that, in order to gain, we have to take from someone who has more. Abundance is, therefore, key to collaboration and partnership. It creates a sense of *win-win*, rather than *win-lose*.

So - in order to create wealth, ask yourself this: what do you want to expand and create more of? What, in fact, do you want less of in your life right now? What kind of life or environment around you will help you to thrive? What do you already have an abundance of?

How do we achieve wealth, prosperity and abundance? We align our values with our money. When our personal values and our money are aligned, we develop new beliefs.

We know now, don't we, that money isn't rational? It's a 'thing' to which we attach all sorts of emotions. And we know that having this emotional connection with money prevents us from having clarity, from having a plan in place. I want you to get that clarity. I want you to have a plan that sticks. With clarity comes motivation and accountability. By the end of this book, I want you to have nailed your mindset and understood more about your personality and your behaviours around money.

Remember - the brain doesn't like anything complicated. It likes everything to be very simple. Tell yourself you're anxious and your brain will look for evidence to support it. When something bad happens in your day and everything else turns into a catastrophe, it's because you've decided it *is* a catastrophe based on your perception: *I've had such a bad day - I've just lost this client and now my car has broken down* ... it just builds and builds until the only way out is to bury ourselves under the duvet and start again the next day, which, by the way, is a perfectly acceptable thing to do!

What if you could change the perception by reframing what you're telling yourself so that your brain will then start to look for evidence to support that instead? Revisit your own story around money as well as stories that have been passed down to you through the generations of your family. Remind yourself of the triggers that cause you to feel emotional around money. Now - consider how to interrupt that cycle by *bringing some consciousness* to it ... think about how to release the negative emotions that are holding you back as well as how to be thankful to them for those times they have served you well and protected you.

A way to get clarity on your financial *present* is to consider what your money situation actually looks like. Imagine you're sitting on the most gorgeous boat on the ocean. It's your job to sail the boat with a specific destination in mind. How much sailing experience do you have? Are you a novice? Are you experienced? Are you at the start of your journey? In the middle? At the end? What are the conditions out there - choppy or calm? What is the condition of your boat? Who do you have on that boat to support you, to give you a helping hand if you need it? Where are you headed? Do you have a satellite navigation system to guide your way? Do you have a life raft for emergencies?

Think of money like a closet or a wardrobe ... you've removed some of the old stuff that no longer serves you, maybe the old shoes in the back that are gathering dust, that don't fit anymore. At the root, money problems are often mindset problems. The greatest financial obstacle that we face is our lack of awareness ... digging out all of that clutter frees us up both physically and emotionally to explore the possibilities that are available to us.

I am going to introduce you to five smaller steps (small steps, big wins!) to work through in this *Create* section:

1. Your Financial Values
2. Get Financially Naked
3. Give every pound a purpose
4. Setting up your pots
5. Conscious financial intentions (over goals)

SMALL STEP #1
YOUR FINANCIAL VALUES

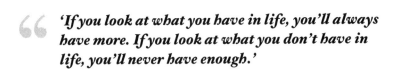

'*If you look at what you have in life, you'll always have more. If you look at what you don't have in life, you'll never have enough.*'

— OPRAH WINFREY

Many of the women I work with expect to walk away at the end of a coaching session with a long list of big, fat, masculine, hairy, financial goals. In my experience, this leads us down a path of exhaustion and burnout. We are not designed to *do, do, do*. In the context of our financial future the most important focus is not the goal, but the alignment of our wealth and personal values. Values are very different from goals – values provide a deep sense of ongoing direction. Goals are what we want to achieve within a certain time.

Annually, around New Year's Eve, my husband and I create a financial plan for the year ahead. The first thing we remind ourselves of is our values ... plus what we desire. We often find we desire quite a few things and find we need to prioritise these! So we concentrate on the three most important desires for ourselves, our family and our children for the next 12 months. We even write them up on our family planning board so we can all see them each day. We break this down into three pillars and one main theme - this year was all about growth. We label each pillar in turn - *personal, business, family* - and then under those three pillars we consider how, financially, we are going to grow our family this year. Financially, how will we grow the business? Financially, how are we going to make sure that we have more time together? Time is the one asset we cannot create more of so this one is super important for us, and I suspect for many. We decided we wanted two family holidays in the summer and so booked them in the knowledge that we had to grow the business in order to pay for them. Our personal growth from spending more time together as a family was a strong financial value for us.

I love choosing a theme as this allows us to consider our current environment, priorities and desires all wrapped up beautifully together to create an expanded idea that is entirely up for discussion.

Activity: *Your financial plan for the year ahead*

Think of a theme you want to focus on for the next 12 months. Think about the kinds of words you could use that are of priority to you right now in your life - words that will encourage expansion. For me, one was *growth*. It was really important for us that we grew as a family, in my business and personally. What would your theme be? What is really important for you?

Draw out three columns headed *Personal, Business, Family* and think of three very clear and specific goals for each of those areas. For example, one thing could be setting up a standing order for £X per month to go into a holiday pot because

you've just saved yourself £X per month by food planning.
That would be a really clear, measurable action. Under your
business column you might decide to plan out your social
media content for the next 30 days. Write the specific action
and underneath that, write the name of somebody who can
hold you accountable.

What emotion comes from this exercise? Fear? Anger?
Shame? Delight? Surprise? I used to beat myself up because of
my overspending on *Amazon* and underwent a lot of self-
discovery during that process to work out why I was spending
so much on picture frames I didn't need. The answer was that
I like memories and I like to store them, and the lightbulb
moment was realising I'd rather have gone on an extra holiday
and spent some time with my family than bought those
frames.

If any of this is triggering for you, that's a good thing -
something is going on in your unconscious mind. Remember -
it is safe to have this awareness for yourself. Try this mantra:
'I am safe and I am getting financially naked to give every
pound a purpose'.

When we feel emotional we should allow our body to process
the feeling, to understand what message it has for us and use
that to help create drive, intention and momentum. If you are
feeling emotional, direct that to an intention or an action to
create change *now*. If that means you need someone in your
boat to support you then go and get that person. If it means
you need to get a little bit tough with yourself, rant at yourself
for five minutes, then do it. This is about moving to action
and change - positive change to get you positive results. It is
in the action that change happens. It may feel scary but
remember that this current situation has been comfortable

for you. We now need to show your unconscious mind that it is safe to stretch your financial comfort zone.

I'll be honest - I did feel really irresponsible. I was a financial expert, I was advising people on how to manage their money every day and I wasn't managing my own. I felt deep shame. So - allow yourself that emotion for just a minute. Think - *what am I going to do differently? How will this serve me? What alternative purpose am I going to give this money? How will this help me to create the financial future I deserve and want?*

You have got this! This is all one hundred percent in your ability. You totally deserve to create wealth, and this is where it all starts.

This exercise is so important because I want you to begin creating financial independence, not *co-dependence*. That doesn't necessarily mean you have to start managing money in your household, but just knowing the numbers could be the next best step for you. As women we need to be in a position of empowerment and awareness because we are living longer than men. Even without managing the household money or getting financially naked, having that awareness is key.

So - if you choose to skip it, I encourage you to do it at a later point, even if you think you have your spending plan sorted. It is an important step on the journey. If you're struggling with it, go back to the *Deserve* section ... and when you feel ready, go again. There are some free resources if you need extra help. Grab them here: *www.itsnotaboutthemoney.com/tools*

CHAPTER 30

DESIRES AND DERAILERS

Values: *Towards* **and** *away from* **motivation**

What are financial values? Values are what you hold to be important in your life, your internal compass if you like. Your core beliefs and values drive how you behave, and your behaviour drives your actions - what you do or don't do. Understanding your values can help to see the importance of meaningful and powerful change.

We have values for every area of our life:

Relationships

Money

Career

Health

Parenting

The values that you place around these areas were formed a very long time ago and have evolved from a combination of influences in your life.

According to sociologist Dr. Morris Massey[1], we each go through three major development stages:

The imprint period (0-7 years): We soak up everything around us. We often take on the values of our parents.

The modelling period (8-14 years): We look for people that appeal to us. We worship heroes. We begin to branch out from our parental bonds a little more.

Socialisation period (15-21 years): We become truly individual. We form peer groups.

Remember - values are very different from goals – values provide a deep sense of ongoing direction; goals are what we want to achieve within a certain time. What do you think is going to motivate you more?

Activity: *Your family values tree*

Take a piece of paper and draw your family tree.

You can use stick people for this if you like. Next to each stick person, I want you to write some singular words to describe that person, e.g. loving, responsible, serious, giving, selfish, greedy, friendly, funny, compassionate, kind, gentle, aggressive. Any word that comes up for you. See how far back in the family tree you can go with this exercise. Ask other family members to help you.

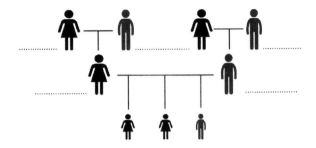

Although you may not be able to ascertain what your family members' financial values were, their behaviour is a glimpse into their values. Perhaps they read a lot. Perhaps they shared their wealth freely. Perhaps they were very careful with money. Behaviour reveals a great deal about what may be going on underneath.

Which of the words you've used to describe members of your family resonate with you about yourself? Which do you think you may have inherited? How has this served you? How has this supported you? How have these values limited you?

Have you ever thought about how these values may need reviewing?

We have two types of values: *towards* values and *away from* values. Values can either motivate us away from pain or towards pleasure.

Activity: *Desires and Derailers*

1 - Draw a line down the centre of a piece of paper. On the left, write the heading *Desires* and on the right - *Derailers*.

Consider the following:

• What do I desire most in my life?
• What could derail me from achieving that?

List your answers under the relevant headings. When you think you have them all, write down another five ... and then five more. Aim to write at least 25 under each heading.

Here are some examples:

What do you desire most?	What could derail you?
Legacy	Selfishness
Travel	Injustice
Freedom	Greed
Creativity	Poverty
Love	Impatience
Joy	Anger
Respect	Confrontation
Resilience	Rudeness
Collaboration	Unsolicited advice
Growth	Criticism
Ease	Being interrupted
Simplicity	Nosiness
Integrity	Ignorance

2 - Rank them in order of priority. Which ones feel the most important to you? Which one would make you feel incongruent or misaligned if you did not live by it? Reduce your list to your top five. (Often, our top three or four values take up most of our time and we prioritise these in order of significance.)

3 - For each area of your life ask yourself these questions using your top five desires:

In relation to my (insert area of life) ... what is important to me about (insert value)?

E.g. In relation to your relationships, what is important to you about freedom? Perhaps you need to have time to create space. Perhaps it is important for you to have two holidays a year to be close to the sea where you can feel free.

In relation to your health, what is important about freedom?

In relation to your career, what is important about freedom?

In relation to your parenting, what is important about freedom?

In relation to your money, what is important about freedom?

In relation to your relationships, what is important about freedom?

4 - Ask yourself, what ways is this present for me in my financial present?

The final step is coming shortly. Don't turn the page just yet.

Now is the time to look at your pleasure and pain motivators, to make sure these values are motivating you rather than keeping you stuck.

CHAPTER 31
PLEASURE AND PAIN

How we make decisions are driven by two forces – pain and pleasure.

Pain keeps us stuck in fear - fear of failure, fear of rejection, fear of pain, fear of judgement from others.

We are either motivated *away* from things that cause pain or *towards* things that create pleasure. We're also motivated towards things that are important to us, that align with our values.

Which do you think is most powerful? Both are!

When we are down in the dumps we struggle to focus on positive things. We know that change is needed but the motivation comes from pain rather than pleasure. As we work on the issue and achieve some change, the 'pain' recedes - and so does the motivation.

Let's go back to the diet analogy. How many times have you said on a Sunday evening: 'Diet starts tomorrow!' You wake up on Monday and begin a new exercise routine or diet. Perhaps you get to Thursday still feeling motivated. Perhaps you achieve a few weeks and see some weight loss - and, right there, you lose motivation. Losing weight was a goal rooted in an *away from pain* motivation, and you've achieved it. The weight comes back on until the pain resurfaces and you begin the cycle again. The same can happen with money.

I want you to tell yourself: 'I always want to be moving **towards** something that will help me feel motivated and in alignment'.

Catherine's story: *Catherine began dipping into her overdraft every month at the age of 18. Her first catalogue account hit its maximum spend and she was able to apply for a credit card with a £500 limit. She slowly reached this and then her bank lovingly offered her the exciting new function of an interest-free £1000 overdraft. 'It's interest-free' she told herself, so she accepted it and continued to spend. Her emotional triggers for overspending against her budget were left unearthed and two years later she was in £30,000 of debt and on a spend-shame-spend-shame cycle. Her financial situation was suffering because she was stuck in the pain cycle, with the pain of feeling bad about her debt fuelling her to pay it off and then losing the motivation as the pain disappeared (only really acting as a short-term motivator) and the cycle continued. When Catherine identified the triggers for her emotional spending, rather than using the pain and shame of being in debt as the motivator, she decided that she was going to focus on the pleasure of saving towards a trip she'd always wanted to go on to the Greek islands. This aligned to her values of freedom and creativity (she'd decided she was going to write a book whilst there) and she redirected every pound she wasn't spending on clothes to this new purpose. Within 19 months she had cleared her credit card debt and published her first book which became a no.1 Amazon best-seller.*

So, pain is a good motivation to get things going, but only in the short-term. As your resolve strengthens with early success, move that motivation to a pleasure or desire focus.

CHAPTER 32
FINANCIAL MOTIVATORS

Does Catherine's story resonate with you?

Are you moving *towards* what you want and desire, or *away* from what you don't want?

Boom! Lightbulb moment!

Are you moving *towards* happiness or *away* from not enoughness, anxiety or fear of loss? Powerful shifts will happen if you take some time to recognise this.

The final step - look again at your list of values and for each one answer these:

1. On a scale of 1-10, how motivated are you towards this value?
2. On a scale of 1-10, how motivated are you away from what you don't want?
3. Where are you spending your time and money?

Time *and* money ... taking both into consideration can reveal so much about what you already value as well as any values conflicts you have. Refer back to your bank statements. Are your spending habits truly in alignment with your values?

How much of your time are you giving away to these values? Are you giving away more of your time to help others? You value love, but if you're giving away time to love others over yourself, this value is not in alignment. Perhaps one of your values is freedom and yet you are a slave to your work, stuck in the belief that you have to work hard to make money. This is not congruent.

There is no point in learning all the practical aspects of how to manage money if you don't have the right beliefs, behaviours and values sitting behind that. Changing habits leads to lifelong change – seriously, that's how I transformed my relationship with money. I am a completely different person. Having racked up £30,000 in debt and robbing Peter to pay Paul whilst teaching others what they should be doing with their money, I was self-sabotaging because I didn't believe in myself. People would tell me how confident I seemed, but that wasn't my story. The moment I changed my habits and beliefs around money, I changed my life.

How we value ourselves is a mirror on how we value the world. Without a sense of self-worth you will find it more difficult to see the world for what it has to offer you. If you don't feel love for yourself, you'll always seek external validation, for somebody else to give that love to you. It's not about the money, it's about *money secrets*. And having money secrets lead to poor focus, heightened anxiety, sadness, worry and deep-rooted shame: I am *not worthy. I'm not good enough.* Money will never give you the happiness you seek – you just want to be loved, and nobody else could give that love to you but yourself. Often, the thing that drives our behaviours and conscious thoughts, whatever it was we didn't have growing up, or what we don't have right now ... well, we could just give that to ourselves. And once we do that, we open up to being able to experience love in a whole different way.

Abigail's story: *Abigail came to me as a highly successful entrepreneur running a health and wellbeing business. She was turning over in excess of £200k per year but her behaviour around money was stuck in a pattern of not enoughness. She and her husband were using their credit card for their day-to-day spend so that they could build up credit card points. However, she had no insight into the spending as the card was in his name and she'd got into the habit of paying herself just enough to pay off the 'debt', as she referred to it, and nothing else. By the time we worked together, Abigail's money belief was that she was in survival (a belief compounded by childhood struggles with being liked and accepted). She felt broke every single month. We acknowledged that the lack of visibility of the credit card spending and the fact she was not paying herself anything over and above kept her feeling broke. As a result, they moved their day-to-day spending to their joint bank account and she set up spending pots, paying herself more than just the amount needed for the bills. We also addressed the cycle of struggle, the struggle that she felt emotionally kept her motivated away from the pain of paying off the debt and towards feeling that it was a worthy challenge. Having set up her pots and given every pound a purpose (see 'small step #3'), Abigail and her husband created a job security pot and within six months he'd joined her business. This switch from struggle to feeling a sense of more than enoughness, purpose and confidence enabled them to change their financial situation.*

SMALL STEP #2
GET FINANCIALLY NAKED

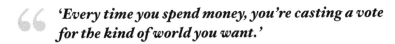

> '*Every time you spend money, you're casting a vote for the kind of world you want.*'
>
> — **ANNE LAPPE**

What??

Yes - *we are going to get naked ... with money* (don't worry - you don't need to literally take your clothes off!) This is about stripping everything back to basics. To know your numbers inside out so that you can build your confidence from a positive place of curiosity and awareness. What gets us more curious than nakedness?!! If this is the step you resist most, take time to check in with how you *feel* when you think about doing this. Remember - money is a physical and emotional journey. Sometimes, it's with the practical steps that we can feel the most resistance. Pay attention to it and journal the hell out of it!

By really understanding your numbers and moving away from financial vagueness, you will be moving into a position of empowerment. It's about being *proactive*, not *reactive* ... and putting you into a position of glorious awareness so that you are back in the driving seat. You are standing in your power.

One of the biggest challenges for women I coach is that they've skipped the basics. They've felt controlled by those old emotions, limited by their old beliefs or the borrowed beliefs of others. So - for many of you this will be scary, particularly if it's your first time. The question to ask yourself, though, is *how will I feel when I begin to let go?* How will you feel when you let some of that financial vagueness go and bring some clarity to yourself? What would be possible for you?

How do you know how much income you need to be bringing in? How clear are you on how much goes out of your accounts every month? How do you manage money? In your boat, if you feel you're a mile from shore, what do you need to be doing to get closer to stability? What is your financial *present?*

Many people believe that the solution to managing your money better at this stage is to create a budget. A budget is an 'estimation of revenue and expenses over a specified future period of time and re-evaluated on a periodic basis' ... zzzzzzzz ... I know, I know, stay with me. Why on earth do you want to 'estimate' money and why on earth do you want to re-evaluate these 'estimates' periodically?? Getting financially naked is not about budgeting or restricting money that you estimate. Who wants to restrict money? *This is about getting crystal clear on what you need to allocate, based on your expected and unexpected needs and wants, to live the life you desire whilst still maintaining balance of present self and future self.* Write that down somewhere.

You are giving every pound a purpose. This is not budgeting!

Activity: *Get financially naked!*

1 - Print off your last three months' bank statements, grab a few highlighter pens (as if we need any excuse to get some yummy stationery out) and place every transaction that comes out of your account into a relevant category. I want you to say the following out loud as you do this (and no skipping this part) - 'I am getting financially naked and giving every pound a purpose.'

And repeat: 'I am getting financially naked and giving every pound a purpose.'

And again: 'I am getting financially naked and giving every pound a purpose.'

As you say this, acknowledge the empowerment you are creating for yourself. Whatever emotion comes up, say: 'I am safe to feel this emotion, I am safe and I am ready to let it go.'

'I am safe to feel this emotion, I am safe and I am ready to let it go.'

'I am safe to feel this emotion, I am safe and I am ready to let it go.'

Don't worry if you feel emotion in your body - this is good. Emotions need to flow. Place your hands on that part of your body and repeat: 'I am safe to feel this emotion, I am safe and I am ready to let it go.' Add in your positive money mantra - the one you created in the *Deserve* section of this book.

Reaffirm that you are safe and that you are loved. You are enough.

I've created a couple of categories for you for this exercise: *fixed costs* and *variable costs.* Fixed costs are regular bills - water, electricity, gas, council tax, subscriptions. Variable costs are things like clothing, haircuts, trips, holidays, car expenses, food - things you *expect* to spend money on, but do not have a fixed amount for.

You can label these into sub-categories if you want: *Household, Children, Lifestyle, Car, Treats,* etc. Total each column up for each month, then, with those three months' bank statements, take an average of each month. Bear in mind that your expenses may be seasonal. You may have higher energy costs in the winter compared to the summer, so add a little extra to these to get your average.

Ask yourself - *what value is each transaction giving me? Can I ditch, switch or turn off?*

2 - Looking at your totals, identify one area to focus on for action.

Just one ...

Create a list of action steps right now. Remember: *Small Steps, Big Wins.* A whole heap of stuff might come out of this. You might identify some direct debits that need cancelling. Perhaps you have too many insurances, or realise that you're overspending on food. Don't make this too overwhelming - focus on just one area. You might, for instance, decide that you need to start saving some money into a savings account for those unexpected emergencies. If you're spending too much on credit cards, now is the time to examine your spending habits. There's a really good app - *Debt Payoff Planner* - in which you can enter the details of your debt and the amount you're paying off and it will give you a debt-free date. You can play around with it. If you have several credit cards you can put in details of each along with the percentage of interest you're paying as well as how much you're paying off every month and it will give you your debt-free day. More on this subject later in the book.

Some of you will take longer to do this exercise and you may have to do it on a few different accounts. Some people have all their bills coming out of a joint account with a separate account for personal spending. At the bank we would encourage joint accounts with salaries paid into personal accounts and a standing order from the joint account to cover all the bills. Whatever's left in your personal account is yours.

3 - Set up your spending plan.

You're still here! Yay! With all of the new clarity you've achieved from the previous steps, you are now empowered to create your meaningful money plan.

First, I want you to take stock of what you have just created for yourself. Ask yourself:

What was I expecting from this exercise?

Were the results what I was expecting?

What does this show me about my current habits?

What have I identified that I want to change?

What have I identified that I want to continue?

Write up a list of three IMMEDIATE actions (e.g. cancel old direct debits/memberships).

Five ways to create your spending plan:

Paper - Use simple columns and categories to help you track. You can use a budget planner, a notepad or a journal.

Simple spreadsheets - you can create your own household spending plan in *Google Sheets*. Also, most banks will now allow you to download your transactions straight into *Excel,* and you can share the document with your partner or money accountability partner.

The Envelope System - As soon as you get paid, withdraw cash and put it in envelopes – one envelope for each category. Once the money in each envelope is gone, it's gone. I really like using this method for areas of overspend. I withdraw a monthly amount and use that to help me get extra focus on saving money in that one area.

The Digital Envelope System - Many digital apps that support the envelope system have been created in the Fintech market, including *YNAB (You need a budget)* and *Starling Bank*[1]. When Starling Bank gained its banking licence in 2016, Anne Boden became the first woman to start a British bank.

The separate accounts method - Similar to the digital envelope system, instead of using apps you use separate accounts, e.g. a bill account, a spending account, a financial security fund account and a tax account.

How do I choose which ones to use?

Think about your money ...

If you are a natural architect, you could think about continuing to embrace that warrior planner in you but counterbalance this by giving yourself some fun money to play with.

If you are a born impulsive warrioress, the thought of a rigid spreadsheet may send you into a state of anxiety! How about using a digital envelope budgeting system with some clever digital banks or apps? Or skimming money each month into a pot for you to have some impulsiveness with.

If you are an enabler, having a separate giving pot for yourself would enable you to feel safe to spend money on yourself - guilt-free.

If you are a pacifist, taking some risks with some of your disposable income may serve you.

If you are an innovator, taking risks comes easier to you and therefore having some controls in place to ensure you do not self-sabotage would be helpful.

Pick one method and stick to it. If it doesn't work, pick another and play with it. Have fun. Stick your favourite music track on and have a regular money date with yourself (more on that in the next section).

Track your spending for 30 days. If 30 days feels too much, track for seven days and just see what happens, what emotions and judgements come up. What triggers you to spend? What triggers you to save? Who influences your financial habits?

Give as much focus to *receiving* money as you do to giving money a purpose

With this new awareness of your money flows, focus as much on your income as your outgoings. There are two reasons for this. First, money needs to flow. Money comes in and money goes out. It's crucial to give as much focus to where it comes from as the purpose we give it.

CHAPTER 33
SO WHY DOES MONEY NEED TO FLOW?

The second reason is that if you focus only on where money flows *from*, you will limit your mindset to feeling comfortable (or uncomfortable!) with giving or spending money. Remember that money is about two things: how comfortable you feel to give and how comfortable you feel to receive. In order to have a balanced, healthy relationship with money, you should focus on inflows and outflows. Whether you are employed or self-employed, focusing on receiving money through varying income sources is exciting! It helps to think about how you can influence the flow of money coming in ... doing so will put your mind into a creative and possibility mindset. When you operate from *flow*, you are able to think more logically and rationally. Have you ever heard yourself say: 'It just does not feel right'? That's your intuition guiding you to a state of positive flow. It is a message to you to trust yourself.

By acknowledging that money needs to flow we are also acknowledging that money needs a purpose, a strong intention. It needs to be given value. Getting financially naked enables us to listen out for these feelings and trust that they are there to guide us towards better financial decisions.

CHAPTER 34
WHAT IS STOPPING YOU FROM BEING IN FLOW?

S ometimes it feels like things just aren't going our way. We get stuck in a rut. In my experience a lot of energy can be wasted focusing on what is going wrong. In order to get back into positive flow, we need to look at what helps us feel at our happiest. Milahy Csikszentmihalyi[1] was a happiness researcher who faced huge adversity as a prisoner in World War II. In his book *'The Psychology of Optimal Experience'* he introduced the concept of *flow* and described is as *'a state in which people are so involved in an activity that nothing else seems to matter; the experience is so enjoyable that people will continue to do it even at great cost, for the sheer sake of doing it.'*

What is interesting to me is what happens in the brain when we are in flow. When we are in flow, the prefrontal cortex, which is responsible for memory, managing emotional reactions and helping us plan, is temporarily deactivated. This inactivation can assist with loss of our inner critic and allow the brain to focus on creativity and possibility. What actually gets in the way of flow are the distraction gremlins - our phones, tv, comparing ourselves to others. When we truly lose ourselves in the moment, the world around us quietens and we achieve things that we never thought possible.

Sawyer (2015) and Kotler (2014)[2] suggested that flow can be sought when all of our attention is focused on the present moment in four specific areas:

1. Social - how we get into flow within a group so that flow can occur together.
2. Creative - thinking differently about the challenges we face and approaching them from a different perspective.
3. Environmental - external qualities in the environment that drive people deeper into the zone.
4. Psychological - internal triggers that create more flow.

Let's apply this to the *Create* stage:

1. Social - Learning about money within a group is incredibly powerful. It is one of the reasons we created group online programmes for women to learn and share together. Who could be *your* flow buddy?
2. Creative - Stepping into gratitude for what you already have can help you see things from a different perspective. Successfully navigating problems, like your limiting money beliefs, will nurture your confidence. So make decisions based on new experiences and challenge those inner self monologues around 'I need to save this money for the future' or 'I surely can't spend that much on this item for myself.' Challenge the unfamiliar.
3. Environmental - When a money decision is perceived to be a threat, we fear the worst, keeping us stuck in familiarity

cycles. Create a rich environment that challenges these comfort zones. Start taking some small risks with your money to gently expand your financial comfort zone. Start an investing club with some friends and your local financial guru to help guide you.

4. Psychological - In order to create flow we should focus on internal prompts that enhance our focus and energy. Create a vision board. Use daily journaling to bring curiosity to those limiting beliefs and avoid setting goals based on external judgement or validation.

A scenario that can move you quickly down from *financial stability* to *financial instability* is being self-employed and neglecting to save for tax and/or VAT in advance.

Linda's story: *Linda was the main wage earner. She worked as a self-employed interior designer contractor. She absolutely loved her job and whilst finding it a big money mindset shift to go from employed to self-employed, she was enjoying making money from her passion. In year one of her business, she made £95,000 in sales and felt proud of her progress. Shortly after her first year in business, after taking into account her expenses, she received her first tax bill of £13,000. She was unable to pay this tax bill and had to borrow money from her parents. This situation caused Linda a huge amount of guilt, shame and fear and within six months she closed her business down and went back to work as an employed designer, feeling that she did not deserve to make any more money. She told herself: 'I am bad at managing money'. Linda and I worked through this money story and she is now once again a self-employed interior designer making twice as much as she ever did, giving every pound a purpose and being more proactive with money. She empowered herself to believe that she could not change the past but she could change her financial future by changing the meaning she gave to money and what had happened.*

Fear, guilt and shame - as we saw in the *Deserve* section of this book - can riddle us with inaction and financial choices that do not serve us. Let's face it - nobody taught us this stuff! Linda had to do a huge amount of forgiveness work before embarking upon the practical steps to recovery.

Activity: *Your 12 month Meaningful Money Map*

The purpose behind this step is to bring curiosity and awareness to what you spend throughout the year.

First step - Once you've analysed your transactions, put them into categories and identify your spending habits, print off a one-page 12-month calendar and map out what happened in each of those 12 months.

What did you spend in January last year? What did you spend in February, March, April, etc? It might be that you had a MOT for your car in February. Maybe you also had car insurance at the same time. Perhaps you hadn't put money aside for that, and it caused difficulty. Perhaps you put it on the credit card.

These are *expected costs*. They may be unexpected in terms of how much, but they are *expected costs*. Every year, we are expected to put our car through a MOT. Every year we generally know that at least one car tyre is going to go through a pothole. We know, realistically, that at least once a year one of our electrical products will fail - dishwasher, washing machine, refrigerator - and occasionally there will be even more catastrophic expenses, such as the household boiler. If you don't have anything set aside for the expenses that will come up for you in the next 12 months, what could you do right now to correct that situation? Could you set up a standing order for just £2 or £3 a week to go into a financial foundations pot?

Christmas is another expected cost. It happens every year, but how many of us put money aside for it earlier than October or November? Or end up paying it off for months after? Yep - that was me too until 10 years ago.

Once you've completed that exercise, the most important step is forward planning. Look forward and think about all the expenses likely to come up again and factor in any new ones. Looking forward is the major difference between budgeting - which is almost always looking back at where our money was spent - and forward thinking. It will move you out of the shame, blame and 'shoulding' mindset very quickly.

From a financial wellbeing perspective, *unexpected* costs cause the biggest financial stress. We need to protect ourselves from that as much as possible. In *Atomic Habits,* James Clear talks about creating new financial habits in order to move from the position you're in now to the position you want to be in. It's so important to have pots set aside so that those unexpected costs don't rock your boat.

I don't think anybody's ever really comfortable about looking at their bank accounts, but the wonderful thing is that it brings so much consciousness (and emotion!)

Susan's story: *When Susan and I worked together, she did exactly that: she looked at her bank account. There followed much guilt and shame about all the money she'd spent on coaches and memberships. She made a commitment to stop spending money this way until she had worked on her money mindset. However, when I asked about the value the courses and memberships provided for her, she agreed that it was very high, but she still felt bad because they were 'big expenses'. This belief came all the way from childhood, when somebody had said to Susan that she 'blew' all of her money. She was still holding on to that belief and choosing to buy expensive things gave her the money message that she was irresponsible with money. This limited her ability to feel comfortable and safe about investing in herself.*

SMALL STEP #3
GIVE EVERY £/$ A PURPOSE

 'There are two ways to get rich - make more or desire less.'

— WARREN BUFFET

Now that you've experienced getting financially naked, become aware of your expenses - money needed today and money needed for tomorrow - it's time to think about giving every pound a purpose. This is my Golden Rule!

So - for each £ or $ you spend I want you to give it a specific purpose. Could it go into an investment pot for children's university fees? Could it go into a tax pot if you haven't set that up yet? Could it go into a treat pot towards that *Eat Pray Love* retreat you've always wanted to go on by yourself (oh, just me then!)? Given your current situation, where could it be best allocated? If you have decided to cancel something that no longer serves you, reallocate it elsewhere. If you don't reallocate and save the money into another pot, you haven't really 'saved' anything! Imagine my little voice shouting 'reallocate' once you have plugged those money leaks.

When analysing your statements, note the variables, e.g if your mortgage ranges between two amounts, give the higher amount to that job and when you don't spend it, put the rest towards one of your other pots. Then start factoring in unexpected costs. What we're doing here is creating a spending plan - such an amazing thing.

Getting financially naked was the first step I took to getting out of my overdraft. It took a while to want to get to that stage as I was fearful, but once I did it, the fear reduced. I looked at my spending habits. I looked at where I was spending money ... I eventually saw that spending £300-400 per month on Amazon wasn't bringing any happiness or value. As a result, I began to question the value I placed on the money I was spending. I also brought some attention to my emotional triggers. What was causing me to spend money? How was I feeling at that moment? I started tracking my finances daily. Every single day, I tracked my numbers. I began to renegotiate my bills and became quite frugal with some of my shopping habits. I set up my first business and then a second. Soon I was earning more money, and with that money I began saving in different pots. Soon I had these pots building up for different purposes. I then decided that every single pound coming in needed a job ... and guess what happened? As the savings in these pots grew, I lost the desire to spend as often - I'd begun to feel, think and behave differently.

That's a whistle stop tour of how I got out of debt (more on this later) and into a very different mindset, but it proves that changing how you're thinking can change your beliefs, actions and behaviours. You can change the ultimate outcome and be where you want to be in the future with more ease.

Reallocating your pounds to different purposes is a complete game changer and you'll be able to deal with those unexpected things from better financial foundations. You can even set up a number of instant access savings accounts that allow you to label your pots. I bank with *Starling Bank* - you can set up pots on your app. The great thing about creating pots is that it uses the principle of mental accounting. We treat money differently depending on the intention. Mentally, if we put money aside for that specific item, we're giving ourselves permission to spend on that item.

CHAPTER 35
IT'S NOT A BUDGET PLAN

Who wants to be limited with their money? - it's actually a spending plan. As soon as you turn the words *budget plan* into *spending plan* the meaning is changed. Just semantics, I know, but it shows the power that the way we feel and the language we use about money has on our mindset. If your financial intention is that *this* pot is for holidays, *this* pot is for your child's university fees, *this* pot is for treat funds, *this* pot is for meals out - the change in meaning changes the way we behave around that particular pot. Mental accounting is powerful.

How much value does what you're spending have against what is valuable to you? If spending £X pounds a month on food is important, that's great because you're allocating pounds to a job that is of high value to you. If you're spending loads on food and food isn't a massive thing for you, if you'd rather spend your money on holidays, something else that needs doing in the house or personal development, reallocate those pounds. And put emotions aside - go in with the intention of getting an idea of where your money leaks are. If your Money StoryTypes™ is *The Impulsive*, your spending habits will expose some leaks you don't want to see but identifying and being honest about them will help you to put your finger on how you feel when making those purchases - and with those two pieces of information you can begin to create change and new habits.

Imagine creating a spending plan that enables you to have the freedom to live the life you want and desire, to manage money within your boundaries, within your comfort zone.

There are so many blogs and things you can read about budgeting. For me, budgeting is about restricting money. You worked really hard to earn that money - why should you have to restrict it? So - when you think about it as a spending plan exercise, how are you allocating your money? Are you giving every pound a purpose? Give every bit of money that comes into your account a job and push back some of those negative beliefs around your spending habits. This is a behavioural change that made the biggest difference for me. It really helped me to stretch that financial comfort zone. If you worry about dipping into your pots you could put them out of sight, out of mind, and move them elsewhere. As for me, I like seeing them. I had enough control to not dip into them. Changing the thought process changes the behaviour. It's when you skip that first bit that you end up dipping into the money and spending it.

SMALL STEP #4

SETTING UP YOUR POTS

 'What you spend is what you value, what you save is what you seek.'

— CATHERINE MORGAN

Back to *Maslow* - I wasn't spending my money on *basic needs*. It was *wants*. Despite earning really good money at the bank, I was still in a place of insecurity and instability because, aside of sick pay, I had no emergency fund. Once I created that emergency pot, the domino effect was amazing. Getting into this new habit motivates you to keep going. Putting just a fiver a month into an emergency pot will build momentum.

Imagine if you gave these pots names, names that mean something other than a rainy day pot or an emergency ... I would encourage a positive name that links to pleasure and away from pain. Here is some inspiration from my community:

Laura's 'Financial security fund'

Vivienne's 'Joyful money'

Skye's 'Safety net'

Jennifer's 'New opportunity fund'

Kate's 'Contingency fund'

Kate's 'My face lift fund'

Darcey's 'Mojo account'

Beverley's 'Live, laugh love' fund

Maria's 'Freedom fund'

Karen's 'Peace of mind' fund

What will you call yours?

CHAPTER 36
HOW MUCH DO I NEED TO KEEP IN THIS POT?

Most financial experts would suggest a minimum of three to six months of living expenses in an account that you can access easily. Have too little and this will bring you back on the pyramid of wealth to a place of instability. Too much, and you will run the risk of holding too much in cash and it being eroded by cost-of-living increases, otherwise known as inflation.

So - this depends on four things:

1. How much do you need? It is important to feel good about money - how much is enough for you to feel financially secure?
2. Are your pots set up and full for unexpected costs?
3. What expenses do you have coming up?
4. What financial foundations do you have in place?

If we use the analogy of a house, building your wealth from strong foundations will ensure your wealth grows as it can be left undisturbed. What constitutes strong foundations for you from a practical perspective?

CHAPTER 37

INSURANCE, WILLS AND FINANCIAL SECURITY POTS

There are several types of insurances to consider, including:

Income Protection

Critical Illness

Life Cover

Business (asset) Protection

I will not attempt to cover all the ins and outs of different types of insurances in this book. It is a topic that is widely covered on the internet and more information can be found over on my blog at www.catherinemorgan.com.

The fundamentals that you need to be aware of are that if your income is protected, you may not require as big a financial foundation pot as someone who is susceptible to a loss of income because they don't have income protection insurance, for example.

If you are in a relationship, I would suggest that you consider having your own financial security fund for independence. I won't be going into all the ins and outs of the tax implications of holding money in joint names or sole names depending on your tax positions and inside leg measurements ... this is about helping you to feel good with money. Please speak with a financial adviser, financial planner or accountant about tax structures. For the purpose of this book, I want to focus your attention on what feels the right amount for you to have to feel empowered.

Activity: *Complete these statements:*

My current financial stability fund is ....

I currently feel .... about my level of stability fund

I want to feel .... about my level of stability fund

My first step is to build it to £...... by...............

My end goal is to have £...... by..................

Remember - the small steps count. Something is better than nothing. If any money gremlins come up for you during this exercise, check in with your money beliefs and tell yourself: 'I am safe, and this is the best next step for me'.

'I am safe, and this is the next best step for me.'

'I am safe, and this is the next best step for me.'

What about a personal development pot? Courses tend to be high-value investments and worth saving for. It's far better to set aside money for personal development than act on emotion and buy one on your credit card.

How about a holiday pot? How much would you normally spend on holidays every year? How much could you be setting aside every month?

We should all have a health and wellbeing pot.

If you're a sole trader or have a limited company, you MUST put money aside from your sales invoicing into a tax pot. The amount will depend on your expenses so speak to your accountant or bookkeeper about this. Don't get caught out as a sole trader. You have to pay tax in advance for the year ahead based on 50% of this year's numbers for the following year (called 'payment on account').

And ... a treat pot. If your Money StoryTypes™ is *The Enabler,* a way to give back to yourself without feeling guilt is to create a non-guilt treat pot that you've completely mentally accounted for. Labelling it your *Guilt-Free* pot or whatever you want to call it will remove that guilt. You give yourself permission to spend money on yourself because it's from a treat fund, not your main bank account. This also applies to the *Architects* out there who find it difficult to spend money on yourselves. Conversely, *Impulsives* and *Pacifists* will find that spending is too easy. Again, by mentally accounting you can give yourself permission for spending on that item you desire. It provides a barrier to overspending. You've compartmentalised that spending. You've allocated that amount to yourself.

Once you start implementing some of these principles, you'll feel more confident. Find an accountability partner if you need help staying on track. Over time, that behaviour will become a new behaviour.

Activity: *Your money pots*

Draw at least five circles or pots and write in those circles or pots what you are going to start saving for, including expected and unexpected costs. If your goal is to spend £1000 on holidays, put that next to your circle or jar. Then put that picture somewhere where you can see it - the more you look at it, the more it will inspire and motivate you to work towards those goals.

How to set up pots if you have a traditional bank account set up

If you are not able to have digital pots, the best way to set these up with a more traditional bank is to simply open up new savings accounts for each of your pots. This may feel excessive, but it will help you to implement the concept of giving every pound a purpose with ease. These days, you don't need to receive paper statements -

this little hack will help you to mentally separate your money for different purposes. It is also a great hack for students to learn when managing money whilst at university or when they start their first job.

CHAPTER 38
THE FRIDGE/FREEZER/LARDER CONCEPT

This is a concept I learned whilst working at the bank. If you struggle to think about where you're allocating money to make sure you're getting the best returns, think of your bank account like your fridge. It's the account you go to pretty much on a day-to-day basis to provide you with food and water. Your larder/pantry/cupboard is where you store your tins, somewhere you go to every now and again. There might even be some herbs stuck in the back of your cupboard from months ago that you can use. These are your regular savings accounts, cash ISAs, maybe children's savings - things that get you a little bit more interest. You won't want to put a lock on that cupboard, but you know how valuable the contents are for saving towards a goal. Your freezer contains items that have been put in for the long-term - like your investments, pension - things we store away for our future self.

Think about your pots - do they need to go in a fridge, freezer or larder? The purpose of your fridge is not to earn high interest. It is for accessibility. If your fridge is nicely stocked, start storing money pots in your larder. Once this feels nice and full, you can work on your freezer.

It can be helpful to think about your fridge, larder and freezer in these timeframes:

Fridge as money for the next 0-3 years

Larder as money for the next 3-5 years

Freezer as money for 5 years and beyond

You can check in with these pots regularly, like you would when you stock up your food cupboards at home.

SMALL STEP #5

CONSCIOUS FINANCIAL INTENTIONS (OVER GOALS)

 'A real sign of progress is when we no longer punish ourselves for our imperfections.'

— **YUNG PUEBLO**

By now, you are beginning to notice and bring curiosity to the thoughts and emotions that drive your money decisions or indecisions. You'll be aware of how you feel when you have to deal with day-to-day decisions around money. You'll recognise, by now, if you're making your money decisions from a place of fear. Conversely, you'll know if you're trying to control the situation, if you're making those decisions from a place of openness and trust in yourself and life. By now, you'll know if you're in a financial fog, if money confuses you, if you experience physical symptoms of financial anxiety. You'll know by now that there is no place for judgement here. You're simply noticing what those feelings are. You'll know that whatever the emotion is - empowerment or disempowerment, shame or pride, inspiration or guilt - in order to create authentic wealth it's crucial to understand these and how they might be blocking you.

Think about your financial intentions and your financial values. If one of your values is, for example, *impact*, then the focus is not on the money but on the impact that you want to make in the world, and one of the by-products of creating an impact in the world is making money. But if the focus for running a business is on the money and not the impact, then the intention is not focused on the value rather than on money. Would that help you to price your services accordingly? Rather than it being about you receiving money is it about receiving that money to do good for the world? What do you want more money for? What would more money allow you to do? More money actually allows you to have more impact!

Perhaps you want financial freedom for yourself. How much would you need to have to feel free? How do you want to impact your clients through the work that you do? If you're employed, how will making more money impact your life both personally and financially? How will it impact your community, or the causes that you support, or the things that you have a real passion for?

CHAPTER 39

WHAT DOES 'BEING GOOD WITH MONEY' MEAN?

Think about two people you consider to be good with money. Write down some words that describe them. These could be people you know, or people you follow - authors, podcasters, mentors, successful people that you've never met ... people like Oprah Winfrey, for instance.

If you were to go to dinner with one of these people you think are great with money, how do you think they would behave? What sort of things would they be doing? What sort of things would they be saying? Thinking? What would their mindset be? If they're a friend or a family member, could you ask them how they feel about money? Could you ask them if they've always felt the same way? Perhaps you've identified somebody and how they feel and you think you want to feel like that. Maybe you've asked yourself why they feel like that and you don't. Perhaps you've identified some things they appear better at, like planning or saving.

What would your world look like if you operated in the same way as one of these individuals? What sort of things would *you* be thinking, doing, saying? For many people, just to visualize or think about what the future would look like with a different thought or belief system around money feels impossible. This exercise, though, has the power to help you to begin that process and to imagine creating real change. Imagine being able to move from instability to stability and from stability to growth and growth to financial independence!

CHAPTER 40
MONEY ALREADY SPENT

L et's talk about money already spent, aka *debt*. This is relevant for you if you have small or large amounts of money already spent, or if you've had debt in the past and a fear of being back in that situation.

I'm going to talk through six common struggles that people have in relation to debt, and three ways that we can focus on how to pay that debt down fast. The importance of talking about some of the common kinds of struggles and challenges in this situation is that if we go straight into the *how* we don't actually face the reality of *why* we get into debt in the first place. If some of these are familiar to you, it will be reassuring to know you're not alone.

So, the first common habit of people who have been, or are currently, in debt is to find the money to start paying it off. In reality, the majority of people in this situation haven't yet got financially naked and gained the financial insight to identify where they're currently spending, where the money is coming from and what could be reallocated towards the debt. Much of this is down to lack of motivation, or shame, leading to money avoidance. If paying that debt off is not a priority, it never will be.

Without insight into what we are spending every month, how can you begin to create a plan to pay that debt back? This part is critical. The next step to getting clarity is to begin finding ways to gain that financial insight into what you're spending.

The second most common challenge I come across is there's no wriggle room.

In essence, there's three choices:

- We spend less.
- We realign our spending to that debt as a priority.
- We make more money.

Ultimately it is about decision and choice, whether that is the choice to go and get a part-time job, ask for a pay rise, reallocate your spending for a period of time or to set up your own little side-line business. What matters most is having a plan, e.g. creating a food plan so that you spend less on food and have more money to allocate towards the debt. *That* is what's going to give you some wriggle room.

The third common challenge is mindset, the regret, remorse and shame of being in that situation. We get into a past money mindset and our narrative often relates to not being able to control it: 'I'm not good enough with money', 'I am terrible with money.' These narratives keep us stuck in no action.

I was in this situation for most of my twenties. I racked up thousands of pounds on credit cards, store cards and loans. Try to recognise that you made a decision in the past that supported your emotional needs at that moment. Or you were ill-prepared for a particular situation, meaning that you had to put money on a credit card, and you've not been able to find any wriggle room since. For many of us in that limiting mindset it can feel so overwhelming. We just think it's too big ... we will never get that debt paid off quickly enough.

By paying off a little bit of that debt every single month, you'll be amazed how quickly it can be cleared - maybe not as quickly as you'd like, but just seeing that reducing total, with small steps, will help you to move away from a lack of mindset to an abundance mindset.

An important element of paying debt down is that if you feel negative and beat yourself up about decisions you've made in the past, perhaps focus on how you can reframe some of those emotions in order to change those behaviours and therefore those habits.

Another common challenge is when money already spent is repaid but then the car breaks down or the washing machine needs repairing or replacing. Money hasn't been saved for this unforeseen situation and the debt resurfaces.

There may always be things that come up that you haven't accounted for early on in your journey. So if your car breaks down next week, and you've just started this process, you may need temporary extra support. Don't be unkind to yourself. It may be necessary to use credit cards and overdrafts for short-term lending needs. The aim is to move you forwards from where you are today.

This also goes for unexpected health issues, when we don't have funds set aside to support our lifestyle expenses. *Catastrophic thinking planning* can be advantageous. What protection policies do you have to replace your income in the event of an accident or sickness? Do you have a pot of money for any adjustments that may be required in your life, for example, someone to collect the children from school? Or a sum of money to cover you in the event of being diagnosed with a critical or serious illness? We dislike talking about catastrophic events but the way I look at it, it's all about getting into a position of empowerment and choice.

If you are employed, you may receive sick pay for a certain period. If you are self-employed, this is something you'd need to get from an insurance broker, financial adviser or on a self-select basis.

CHAPTER 41
DO I SAVE OR PAY OFF DEBT FIRST?

W hich do I do first? There is no right or wrong answer to this. Some financial experts say you must pay down debt as quickly as possible before building an emergency fund. There's another school of thought that says if you just focus on paying off debt without having an emergency fund in place, in the event of a catastrophe, you end up creating more debt.

My belief is that if you build a financial security fund first you are more likely to future proof yourself against unexpected costs and increasing debt. Also, saving money is more motivating than being stuck in negative cash flow, leading to a poverty mindset. Even if it's £500, having a little bit of a cushion behind you is empowering.

The final challenge I hear about a lot is something called *comparisonitis*. We constantly compare ourselves to everybody else. We make ourselves feel bad about our own decisions. It sounds crazy, doesn't it, when you read it like that? How can someone else's life actually make us feel bad about our own life? This creates a lack of gratitude, and do you know what? Who cares about Mr and Mrs bloody Jones! I definitely lived my 20s comparing myself to other people and wondering what people think about me. That is not a healthy habit. Why? Because although it is natural human behaviour to compare, it also sets expectations and ignores the issue of different values and priorities. If we try to replicate other people's spending habits, we ignore our own needs.

CHAPTER 42
3 WAYS TO TACKLE MONEY ALREADY SPENT (DEBT)

One of the best concepts for tackling money already spent is snowballing. The debt snowball method was originally made popular by personal finance expert Dave Ramsey[1]. *Snowballing* - paying off the smallest debt you have first (excluding your mortgage), giving you a boost of motivation to pay off the other, larger debts. Once your smallest debt is paid off, you have some money to allocate towards your next smallest debt. You pay that off, and then allocate that money to the next part. It's a valuable concept because it makes it easier for you to achieve smaller goals and rewarding yourself for doing so. It creates a mindset of empowerment.

The second method is the *avalanche,* where you focus on paying off the one that's got the highest interest rate first. So - if your credit card has a 28.9% interest rate and your overdraft is 11.9%, you would pay off the credit card first.

Once you have decided which method you want to adopt, the next most important step is to create for yourself a *debt free date*. Google *snowball calculators* and work out, based on your payments, when you will be debt-free. Then, each time you pay off one of your debts, celebrate! Cut the card up and celebrate the hell out of your achievement!

The third way to pay debt down fast is to consider debt consolidation with an unsecured loan. This is quite popular and simple to do. Typically, you'll have a fixed interest rate set over a number of years and one fixed monthly payment. This is helpful from a budgeting perspective, and you can add that into your spending plan. You also have a set date for when that debt will be paid. The disadvantage is that this doesn't necessarily change your financial habits, and over the longer term, as you're spreading that debt over a longer period, you may end up paying more back than you would have done if you'd used one of the snowball methods.

Another popular debt consolidation method is to secure it against a property, often your main residence. This is known as a secured loan. Adding it to your mortgage and spreading it over a longer period can help with affordability but again, the longer you're spreading that debt over, the more you're paying back. Sometimes it isn't about how much you're paying back. Sometimes it's about creating a clean slate, getting good habits in place so that you don't get into that situation again and forgiving yourself for decisions that you've made. My recommendation would be to find a really good independent mortgage advisor who will talk you through your options and give you recommendations for what's best for you.

A kind word here ... if you're in significant debt and it's causing you significant problems, there are some fantastic debt organisations, such as Step Change, who have some great tools on their website that you can use 24 hours a day, and helplines for people who need debt counselling or to create debt strategy plans. You may even find some that are more local to your area. It can be great to have conversations with these organisations because they're very used to dealing with people in these situations, situations that can arise through no fault of your own - a relationship breakdown, a narcissistic marriage, financial abuse or loss of a loved one.

It's all about balancing the pros and cons of different approaches and finding something that works for you. Think about what's going to fit in with your spending plan, how much can you afford, how much you are going to prioritise and how it will support your mindset.

And bring the solution back to your relationship with money. If you know you're an impulsive spender, then perhaps not having a credit card is the best thing for you. Or keep one credit card for when you're going to travel abroad, but stick it in the freezer until the summer months when you can defrost it and use it. Or take your credit card details off the websites that you commonly shop on. Filter out marketing emails that cause you to spend impulsively. Put them into a separate email folder so that they're still there but you can choose to look at them when you are in a rational mindset. Implementing a 48-hour cooling off period is also very clever. Put something into your online shopping basket and leave it there for two days. If, after two days, you go back and really, really need that item, and if it can be factored into your spending plan, check it out. I lost track of the number of times I forgot to even go back to the basket because I'd decided in the meantime that I either couldn't afford it or didn't need it. It's giving yourself that time to act rationally rather than emotionally. It allows the brain to have that time to think about the decision and it takes the emotion away from the decision. Think about when you are making important financial decisions - during the week, when you're super busy and stressed, when time is an issue. Can you see how vulnerable this makes you to impulsive emotional decisions around money? And making decisions about money at a time when you're highly emotional is never a good thing to do. Take *Black Friday*, wholly designed to play and pull on those emotional strings. If you're looking forward to *Black Friday* this year, and I know that many of you will be, make a list of things you actually need. And stick to that list. Don't be tempted by marketing emails and offers that are going to pull you into impulsive buying - step back and think *what do I actually really, really need?*

Your path to financial freedom can be broken down into very specific intentions or goals. Having a goal in place is important because it gives you something to work towards. You're more likely to do it if you set yourself a daily goal. It builds momentum.

I'm a huge believer in consistent growth so a goal for me every single day is to learn something new. I read a lot, listen to a lot of podcasts and invest in personal development because I believe that will help me climb the ladder of wealth. I have a pot of money for self-actualization (*Maslow*) and use that pot to invest in coaches, mentors, courses and retreats. There's a difference between doing those things in order to tick the self-actualization box versus doing them because you have this fear that you're not good enough.

When you create goals and have a plan, you need to make sure that these stick, otherwise it's just good intentions and no action. I've heard it so often from clients: 'I've got all these good intentions ... I think I know what I'm doing, but when it comes to doing it, it just doesn't happen. Why is that?' Well, it's because of your habits and your behaviours. It's because your money story is not about the money at all - it's about the relationship you have with your money.

Focus on things you can control. This will give you the confidence to get clear on how to create financial goals and financial intentions. I'm an *intention over goals* fan because goals are finite in time. Create intentions and take it from intention to action. Get started on your journey - do one thing each day - and get perfect later. Perfectionism keeps us stuck in poverty.

CHAPTER 43
REFRAMING DEBT

Debt has become a dirty word. As a society we attribute a lot of blame and shame to debt ... economic debt, student debt, credit card debt. In reality, debt is a necessary flow of money to enable the economy to grow. There are many times we can use debt or borrowing to help grow our businesses or invest in our future.

The challenge arises when we use debt to fulfil our basic needs. A debt is essentially borrowing against our future self and if you're using debt to meet basic needs it could well be that you just *have* to do that. However, when you are using debt to meet some of those higher needs - a course for £10,000 for example - you may need to think again.

The emotional issues that debt can present can have a huge impact on how we feel. Denial of our financial situation can lead to further debt and burying our heads in the sand. We don't want to deal with the shame of debt. This denial can then lead to a feeling of regret. We tell ourselves that we should have saved the money instead or we should have better money behaviours. We 'should' on ourselves. This leads to the 'what ifs'. What if I can't pay it off? What if I can't get another job? It puts added pressure on our personal relationships and our own mental health.

Paying off this debt can bring emotional freedom - *away* from the stress, fear, denial and shame. The emotion of debt we carry in our heads will have power over the decisions we make with money.

Change your language

In order to foster a positive relationship with money let's first of all reframe debt as 'money already spent.' The decisions you have made have been and gone. They are in your financial past. Use the exercises in the *Deserve* section of this book to practise forgiveness of your past money decisions. It is now about looking forward to creating positive changes. We can't do that if we continue to hold on to the shame.

Identify the words you use around debt. What do you notice? Do you use expressions like: 'I am bad with money;' 'I am drowning in debt.' These words hold such a lot of power. Is what you are saying really true? Are you really 'broke?' Could a change in the way you manage money help you to feel less broke?

The unconscious mind does not know how to distinguish between truth and non-truth and the language you use becomes its truth. Chat with a friend and ask them to listen to your language around money. Think about the patterns of this language, the stories it's locking you into.

I once hosted an online money date meeting in my Money Circle® and one of the members said: 'Catherine, I hear you saying that in order for you to charge more you have to give more.' It was another lightbulb moment for me. I recognised that in order for me to feel deserving I also had to feel like I was giving. Consequently, I only charged more when I was giving more. Another member described how at school her teacher used to say 'sharing is caring', so she came to believe that she had to share her money, otherwise she perceived herself to be uncaring. You can break the pattern of repeating these stories and narratives by acknowledging that they may not be serving you and may be acting as disablers and derailers.

Replace any disabling words with enabling words. Try using the word *'and'* at the end of each of your sentences, e.g. 'I am drowning in debt, *and* I am committed to learning how to change my relationship with money.' 'I am bad with money, *and* I am making the changes I need to feel confident about it.'

Activity: *Explore your relationship with debt*

In the last year have you made a purchase on your credit card without considering how you will pay this off?

What experiences have you had around debt growing up?

Do you feel in charge of your debt?

What emotions do you carry around debt?

Is debt an enabler or a disabler for you?

What do you hear yourself saying about debt?

What language do you use around debt?

Sometimes debt can come from other people in a relationship. Let's explore why conflict comes up and how we can deal with this.

CHAPTER 44

FINANCIAL CONFLICT - WHY DOES IT HAPPEN?

W hat is the biggest unresolved issue that couples face? Money. Why? As we learned in the *Deserve* section, it's because of a clash in the *meaning* that we attach to money based on our own borrowed beliefs. We have grown up with different experiences influencing our beliefs and perceptions. This next sentence will blow your mind ... Did you know that we are almost always attracted to our financial opposite? Yep, that's right. As an *Architect*, we are attracted to *The Impulsive*. This is exactly what it is like in my household. My husband is The Architect and I am The Impulsive. The irony of the financial planner, I know! You can see how this can create three main conflicts:

1. Money secrets
2. Money shame
3. Money infidelity

So, what is the solution?

Two things: building trust and understanding your values. A lot of people don't realise that they are spending money in conflict with their values. When you align the way you spend, save, invest and give with your values, you'll have a much more purposeful life. It's not really about the money, is it?

Remember you are two individuals coming together, not one couple expected to agree on everything. We have to be mindful of our own beliefs around money so as not to create expectations that one of us is right and one of us is wrong. Remember that financial comfort zone exercise from the *Deserve* section of the book? One of you may be more comfortable with less whilst the other more. Sometimes one partner has a wider range of comfort zones and is more comfortable with both more or less.

It can help to create funny money characters in your relationship. By separating out the part of us that gets offended or feels some clash, it can help us to take a new perspective. We have Elvis and Gertrude in our house!

Speak to the character as if it were a person and talk as if you are trying to assist with the other 'money person' in your relationship (who may be causing some tension in your financial conversations): *'Elvis thinks that it is important to go on that holiday because he is exhausted and time is something he needs right now.'*

'Getrude thinks this is reasonable but could Elvis consider this hotel as an alternative to ensure he still gets that time away but that it does not break the spending plan budget?'

CHAPTER 45

NAVIGATING MONEY IN A RELATIONSHIP

 'I can live without money but I cannot live without love.'

— JUDY GARLAND

Having a money date with your partner - talking about it
So you have just created your desires list and then BOOM! Just when you think you are making progress, your partner storms in with a completely different idea. Conflicts around money are so common in relationships, in friendships, with spouses, partners, family members. The most important thing to remember is that each individual on the planet has their own unique relationship with money. It's the different meanings and perceptions that we hold around money that create the conflict, not that one of you is wrong and one is right. One of the hardest things about talking to your partner about money is the actual communication part of finances in order to start making some progress.

In order to have positive communication with your partner about money, you both need to be willing and open to the conversation. There also needs to be some level of agreement in terms of what's going to happen next. I won't sugar coat this topic. I can't say that you won't go through some tough, uncomfortable, perhaps awkward conversations with your partner about money. It's entirely normal.

Tip 1 – Understand your starting point

Understand where you're both starting from in your relationship to money. Is one of you a natural architect, enabler, impulsive? Disagreements are unlikely to be about money itself. Often, they're about a simple clash of values.

Tip 2 – Get curious

A question I recommend for anybody looking to have a more positive financial relationship is to ask your partner what their earliest memory of money is. This will help you to identify their money story, address the conflicts and negotiate some alternative choices and decisions. What did they hear or not hear about money growing up? What beliefs do they have about money?

Tip 3 – Set specific roles

Create a list of roles and responsibilities, but always be aware of your differing values.

Tip 4 – Take it outside

People always make progress when they have either accountability or others supporting them in their journey, not just their partner. Having a financial friend outside of your relationship can help you to make additional progress.

Tip 5 – Personal goals

Have separate *and* joint financial goals. You don't need anybody's permission, just your own money pots.

CHAPTER 46

THE STRONG MODEL TO BUILD
FINANCIAL TRUST

If you consider that conflict happens because of a clash in the meaning you attach to money, you can begin to think about how to harbour stronger and more positive conversations to balance out your money superpowers and your own money narratives. You can then use this to teach your children, grandchildren and every single future generation ahead of you. We should build STRONG, *healthy conversations:*

SHARE   TALK   RESPONSIBILITY OPENNESS NEGOTIATE GROW

Share
Talk
Responsibility
Openness
Negotiate
Grow (and Repeat)

Share

The emotions we feel when we talk about money create situations in our minds, all based on the stories that we tell ourselves. These stories are from the past. Events that have already happened. Stories are incredibly powerful but here's the thing: they actually stop us from being present in the moment, the here and now. When these stories are different for the person we are talking to about money, they create conflict.

University College London (UCL)[1] conducted a study that involved recording the brain activity of 21 pairs of volunteers. The results confirmed that the human brain undergoes a range of reactions when we find our beliefs are challenged. The study focused on something that will always spark strong opinions – the value of real estate or property.

The volunteers were paired up and showed images of properties. They were asked to assign a financial value to each one. They were then asked to put their (metaphorical) money where their mouth is. They were expected to wager a theoretical cash sum on the strength of their convictions.

Although the duos were separated by glass, they could each see what value their partner had assigned. Brain activity was monitored throughout the process – most notably the prefrontal cortex. This is the part of the brain that focuses on complex decision-making and social behaviours. This part of the brain also reflects the confidence we feel in a decision-making partner. When the two parties agreed with each other, this was reflected in their brainwaves.

The results showed a form of *confirmation bias*, with each volunteer buoyed on by the sense of agreement. This led to them growing increasingly bold in their assignments of value. When the volunteers disagreed with each other, the brainwaves stopped tracking any kind of confidence. It closed down completely, disregarding the possibility that an opposing viewpoint was worth considering.

While the human brain is more than happy to be told that it's right – and to accept the dopamine rewards that come with that – it seemingly refuses to accept the idea that it could be wrong - the 'la la la I am not listening' moment.

The moderators of the study quizzed the participants afterwards. It was confirmed that they heard, acknowledged and remembered the opinions of their partner. They were just not prepared to give the viewpoint any weight.

So, we *can* listen but often choose not to.

It is important here to just be aware. Imagine the brain is like a glass of water. It gets fuller and fuller. We need to wait for it to start to come down before we can begin to have a rational conversation, which is why timing and creating a space where both people can speak and be heard is so important. Perhaps you could have a money spoon and whenever that person is holding that spoon, the other person needs to listen and not speak. Bide yourself some time if you feel your emotional glass filling up by asking a simple question of your partner like: *'That's interesting. Tell me a bit more about that...'*

Start with curiosity. Clear any emotional feelings that stop you from being present and talk.

Talk

Talking about money is really talking about your needs and values. What are your individual values aside from those in your relationship? Refer to the **Small Step #1 - Your Financial Values** *section* of the book to get some clarity on this. When you communicate your needs and values, it is important to use collaborative language. Here is an example:

'What I heard you say was....'

'Would you consider this as an alternative?'

'I am willing to do this. How about you?'

If you come to the conversation from a collaborative perspective, you are more likely to reach some small, shared agreements. You can then summarise these into a 'shared agreement' document. Type this out together. Put it on your fridge. Add it to the top of your spending plan.

Responsibility

Disagreements around money can also occur when someone in the relationship refuses to take ownership of the *doing* tasks.

Before we can take responsibility for the action steps around money, we also need to let go of shame and blame. You both have to put on your 'No shame, No blame' hats. That doesn't mean not having any guilt or not taking any responsibility. It just means *no shame, no blame*. There's a big difference. We can still love one another and disagree with each other. '*I love and respect what you think here, but this is what is important to me. Is there a way we could come to a decision that helps us both feel valued and meets both of our needs?*'

Just because one of you earns more than the other, or one of you has historically managed the money in the home, do not think that this should be the right way. Remember there is no 'shoulding' here! I believe strongly that it is important for the couple to have shared responsibilities, particularly when it is highly likely that women, due to living longer, will have to manage money for longer. It's important to share the responsibility of household money management, not just the day-to-day money but also the bigger financial decisions like investing. It's incredible to think that it was not until the 1960's that women could actually even open their own bank account!

Openness

 'Seek first to be understood then to understand.'

— **STEPHEN COVEY**

If your partner reacts negatively every time you mention money, it may be because they have never been given permission to express how they feel safely. They feel it's unsafe territory because it's *always* been unsafe territory. One of the greatest gifts you can give each other is space. Be open to listen to each other's needs. Think about timing. Pay attention to one another's energy levels. Choose your moment - set aside some time when you are both away from stressful environments. Talking about money when you are emotionally flooded or stressed never produces positive conversations. Consider the topic carefully, too. If the spending conversation historically brings up disagreements, start with something a little gentler. For example, *'I was listening to a podcast episode the other day about lessons we learn from our parents, and I got curious to what lessons we may have learned. What comes up for you when you think about this?'*

Be curious about each other's needs. It is ok to have different needs, after all we are human and individual. *'What is important to you when it comes to how we use money in our life?' 'How will you know when this need is being met?'*

Consider which boundaries need to be in place for you to honour each other's needs. Boundaries are what you can tolerate without it moving to a place where you feel out of alignment from your own personal values.

When you feel like your output of energy and resources is greater than your input for an extended period of time, boundaries are necessary to keep the peace.

Negotiate

Acknowledge now that there will be areas you'll need to negotiate, because you won't agree on everything. Have some alternatives or counter offers up your sleeve. Try enforcing your boundaries by giving some *soft* rejections or alternatives like:

'I'd like to honour your needs here by bringing the family out for dinner, but I'm a bit tight on money this month. What about [next proposed date] instead

or how about we don't have that takeaway tonight and reallocate the money towards this?'

'Maybe we can meet in the middle and come to a compromise that works for both of us.'

'Before we invest the entire amount, how about we invest half of it in this fund and keep the other back in cash, then review it in three months' time once I have built some confidence in investing?'

Grow (and Repeat)

Write your shared agreements down. It is much more powerful to commit to something in writing. There begins a deep phenomenon that happens when we write things down - *encoding*. Encoding is the biological process by which the things we perceive travel to our brain's hippocampus where they're analysed. From there, our decisions are made about what gets stored in our long-term memory and, in turn, what gets discarded. Writing improves that encoding process. In other words, when you write it down it has a much greater chance of being remembered.

When you write your agreements, focus on the behaviours. What behavioural change are you each seeking? Perhaps it's an improvement on the amount of money you save or an improvement on spending on your own needs without feeling guilty. You could create an 'emotional money barometer' to measure the progress of your money emotions and discuss them over a glass of wine.

Select a specific date and time to review, remembering to check in on each other's energy levels first and rearranging if the time does not feel right. Adding the date to the diary, though, is important to solidify the intention of future actions.

In order to grow together financially, you also need motivation. Find a mutual driving force. Give yourselves a reward for the next time you review your progress. Upgrade the wine for the next money conversation perhaps?

When you prepare for your next conversation, ask yourself as well as *what* you need, *who* do you need? Who can you have on your financial empowerment team? A money coach, a financial adviser, or even just a third party? When I have worked with couples, being that third party in the conversation can be incredibly powerful to encourage the follow-through of the STRONG model.

CHAPTER 47
MOVING FROM CREATE TO GROW

Okay, so you've de-weeded everything. You've removed beliefs, thoughts, emotions and behaviours that don't serve you. You've even been able to thank some of the difficult emotions you've experienced for protecting you from behaviours, thoughts and actions that might have been disastrous for you. You've revisited your financial past and rewritten your money story. Now that you're armed with these new financial beliefs and behaviours, what of the future?

It's great to look at our financial past and think about our behaviour and our emotions around money, but to create any change we should look forwards. We should make sure that if we're going to meet any storms on our boat, we are able to manage that situation.

Visualize yourself in that boat. What direction are you headed in? What stage of wealth creation are you at? If you're at *esteem* or *self-actualization* then perhaps you're in a bigger boat and you've got everybody on your team and you're all rowing together in the same direction.

Through the lens of *Maslow's Hierarchy of Needs* you've assessed the conditions of your sea and now it's about focusing on resilience, getting in your lane and staying there. The next step is to see how you can begin to build more stability in your ship and calm those waters!

'*Earn with your mind, not your time.*'

— **NAVAL RAVIKANT**

CHAPTER 48
GET EMPOWERED

Welcome to your financial future!

It's time to feel safe, deserving and empowered to grow your wealth. It's time to have more money, to keep it and to grow it. By now, we have learned how to deserve more and create more money by exploring our relationship with it through a trauma-informed lens, managing what we do create well and holding onto more of it. But how do we grow it?

I won't be covering investment options in this section (that's another book!) or dive into the stock market or property investment, despite those being passions of mine. Instead, I'll be focusing on how to continue momentum and climb the wealth stages from Financial Security to Financial Growth and towards Financial Freedom - freedom from self-limiting beliefs; freedom from borrowed beliefs that keep us stuck in fawning, and freedom to Step into Wealth®.

So why is it so blinkin' hard for women to have more money?

First, let's reflect on the narratives we choose to use with ourselves that are specific to growing our wealth. The most common one I hear is this: 'I am broke'. This belief keeps us stuck in trying to *create* more money, so we rarely ever get to *grow* more of it.

I need you to hear one thing right now: *You are not broke*.

When we see ourselves as 'broke' we ignore or devalue the money we do have and how we choose to allocate it. How many times do you hear yourself saying 'I am broke'?

I am broke infers a lack of money which, in turn, connects to your sense of self. When we choose to use these words, we are expressing money based on how we feel about ourselves.

I am broke.

I am bad at managing money.

I am terrible at maths.

The language we use about ourselves is powerful. Our brains take every word as an instruction to find more evidence to support a core belief. Rather than limiting ourselves to the mindset of *lack of,* or *not enoughness*, we can choose to reframe our language.

'I am choosing to spend my money in another way' ... *for a different purpose.*

Can you hear the difference?

Words matter when it comes to expressing your relationship with money and your relationship with yourself. Choose words that evoke positivity and empowerment.

You're not broke(n).

You matter.

CHAPTER 49
WEALTH EMPOWERMENT

F inancial opportunities and financial challenges both exist for
women now, greater than ever before. It isn't always about
having more, though. For me, growing wealth is about having the
right mindset, beliefs and behaviours in place so that you can
comfortably accept money in, hold on to money and give it with love
whilst maintaining your own boundaries and needs. It is not all about
the big hairy masculine goals that we have been taught are
important. Knowing how to deserve, keep and grow wealth is where
we can create more empowerment, confidence and resilience. To *be*
wealth, to *have* wealth and to *do* wealth.

When I created my first online investing course in 2019 to help
women get started in investing and navigate the jargon surrounding
the stock market, students confirmed that it wasn't just the financial
knowledge that set them off on their journey to creating wealth, but
the change in belief and the automation of new habits they adopted.
No longer did they believe that investing was just for the wealthy, or
that it was too late to start. You can invest with just £1.

And you now know about the power of developing new habits,
creating positive money stories and adopting beliefs that serve you.

In this section you will work on the small steps required to move you from your current financial situation and closer to your financial future ... so that you can feel better, do better and be better. You are ready for this!

The first step to being wealthy is to see it, feel it and believe it. In order to step into wealth®, you have to want it. To desire it. That may seem absurd but so many women don't believe that they are even capable of being that wealthy woman.

You may often wonder why you are not taking any action in creating the future you know you want. You procrastinate, you worry, you are anxious about it, right? What if I told you that the reason you take no action is that your brain is stopping you? The brain doesn't like uncertainty and, of course, the future is full of that.

Begin acting as if you are already living as that future you. The brain cannot differentiate between fact and fiction, so the process of visualising ideas creates the same biochemical reactions and feelings as if you were to have experienced it in real life already.

By creating a vision of your future self in the present moment, you are helping your brain to create this feeling *now*. You will create new neural pathways, new experiences, new thoughts and new beliefs, and your brain will hold on to these.

Many of us find it hard to visualise the future. It is too disconnected from the here and now, and often generates a feeling of lack or deprivation. Our unconscious mind may intervene by saying something like 'That will never happen' which, in turn, manifests the exact circumstance that resonates with the frequency of impossibility. This can cause resistance to the wealth we desire and deserve in life.

So - instead of reflecting on the past, reflect on the future. Create new possibilities. Check, also, that your current self is on the right path and has set the right intentions.

Before we do this together, I want you to complete the 'Step into Wealth® exercise.'

CHAPTER 50
STEP INTO WEALTH ® - PART 1

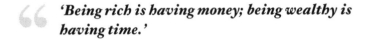

'Being rich is having money; being wealthy is having time.'

— **MARGARET BONNANO**

Close your eyes and recall a memory from your recent past. You might wish to download the audio exercise from *www.itsnotaboutthemoney.com/tools* Recall something that happened in the last two years, something where you wanted money but were not ready to receive. Perhaps it was a conversation with a boss about a pay rise, or a business launch that didn't go as you wanted. Imagine the amount of money you desired and what you would be doing with it now. It's not important how real or delusional this might feel but take the time to see it as being real. To feel it. To see it. To hear yourself. Totally immerse yourself in that vision of stepping into wealth. Step right into that picture. Step Into Wealth right now.

Imagine that scene again as if it were playing like a movie, but this time you are the director. Imagine yourself celebrating the pay rise or the launch of your dreams. Perhaps it has nothing to do with money and you are stepping into your perfect health or your perfect relationship. Perhaps you have just arrived in one of the countries on your vision board. Bring in some other people to the scene. Who is celebrating with you? Who have you taken away from the scene? Perhaps some people were draining your energy, telling you that you could not be successful. Imagine the weather. Is it hot? Are you wrapped up in a cosy blanket somewhere? What can you see around you? What can you smell? Your favourite perfume? A candle you are burning. Now bring in some colour - colour that represents wealth to you. Bring in items of that colour - a necklace, a crystal, trees, clothes - anything you desire. Now imagine increasing the intensity of that colour. Intensify the sounds. Intensify the feeling that comes up for you. What is that emotion? Step into that right now. Feel it come inside your heart and send it out to every cell in your body, every muscle, all the way through your head, face, neck, shoulders, chest, arms, down your fingers, into your lungs, down your tummy, your pelvis, your legs, to your knees and out through the feet into the earth. You are sending it out into the earth, to the rest of the world.

Open your eyes.

Write down what came up for you.

- What do you need to feel from today and every day forward in order to Step into Wealth®?
- Who do you need around you?
- Who do you need to remove or pay no attention to?
- What do you need to forgive?

So - what if you now asked yourself to send your future self a message? What do you think you would say? Let's try a visualising exercise to help your current self to Step into Wealth® in the future.

CHAPTER 51
STEP INTO WEALTH ® PART 2

You are celebrating your 90th birthday. You open the door to the gorgeous cottage you've rented by the sea.

What do you notice?

What do you see?

Who is with you?

What qualities does this 90-year-old version of you possess?

What has she done that you are proud of?

What has she left behind?

What are people saying about her?

Step right into your future. Notice what it looks, sounds and smells like. What are you saying about yourself?

Now imagine your future self tapping you on the shoulder. You turn to find her looking at you with so much love. She has a message for you. What does she say? Can you hear her or is it more of a feeling? What does she want you to know? What does she want more of in her life? What does she want less of? Which part of *you* is speaking to you?

Spend 15 minutes writing this down before moving on.

Now that you have this important message from your future self, you can begin to think about the actions you will take to create that future. You must do this work first because if you don't, you will simply create more of the past. Just read that again: *you will simply create more of the past.* What elements of your past do you want to continue? What elements do you want to change? Your brain loves to repeat the past - it is familiar, and this creates certainty and security in the mind. Your unconscious mind does not know that the uncertainty of getting a new job or setting up a pension for yourself isn't going to kill you. It thinks that anything new and different is dangerous. When you think about your future self you are pulling from your imagination and intuition something that your brain hasn't yet experienced.

So bring it to life! Make it exciting. Bring some colour into it. Some smells, visual cues, even some tastes. Create a *Pinterest* board and pin pictures of your future life (not those old-fashioned images of park benches and golf!) Decide on a date by which you want this and add it to your board. Keep it somewhere you can see it. Add your money mantra affirmations to it. I like to keep a candle on my desk that smells of the sea and a potted cherry blossom tree to remind me of growth and beauty. By representing your future self through images you will begin to stimulate emotions that are connected with the moments. You could increase the motivation by creating a *Current and Future Me* board. On the left, place images of your current life, everything you are grateful for right now. On the right, place the images that represent your future self. You may find that some guilt and shame comes up here ... and guilt can stop you from moving forward with this exercise. Remember - more often than not, negative beliefs contribute to unhealthy financial behaviour. Change occurs most readily when you recognise where this guilt is coming from and begin to practise deep self-love. If this feels too hard, revisit the *Deserve* section of this book.

This is a great exercise to do at the start of the year. I often use it at the start of each season.

*Remember this whenever you are in future planning mode: it's all about being fully present **now**, whilst thinking of a very deliberate and intentional future.*

Expand your vision - The Two Powerful Questions

Now that you are clearer on this vision for yourself, imagine the possibilities for expanding it to your life vision.

Ask your present self two powerful questions to help you become clear on your life's vision and purpose:

1. What impact do I want to create and what expectations do I have for my life vision?

2. What impact do I want to create without any expectation? (your life purpose.)

Let me bust a myth ... your life's vision is not about you. If your life's vision is only about yourself you need to expand expand expand! It is about the impact you want to create in the world, in your communities, in your circles. But don't limit yourself. Go big! Your life's vision is not about buying a bigger house or visiting somewhere in the world. Think big. Think global. What change do you want to see in the world? What are you unlikely to ever attain? What is unmeasurable? Your life's purpose is the impact you want to create but without any expectation for it.

My friend and podcast guest Suzy Ashworth asked me four questions that she referred to as the *inevitable ladder*. In order to expand your vision, ask yourself:

What is a potential vision?

What is a possible vision?

What is a possible vision for me?

What is inevitable?

The third question was profoundly powerful for me. I had been limiting myself by focusing my vision on empowering one million women to be financially resilient. The following day I removed the one million number from my vision board.

What often stops us from thinking big here are our own limitations based on our fears. The most common fears that come up are:

1. Fear of success and/or
2. Fear of failure.

Fear is a powerful limiting emotion caused by the belief that somehow, we are threatened. But really fear is of the unknown, the unfamiliar. The thought of having more wealth in money may feel fearful because it is unfamiliar. When we feel fear of failure or success, we avoid starting businesses, we do not believe in ourselves and will not reach our potential.

Our brain perceives fear of failure as shame and embarrassment to others. If you think about it, does failure actually ever exist? The only reason we feel we have failed is that we haven't met the expectations put on us by ourselves or others.

One way to deal with fear is by focusing on the emotional benefits of your financial goals rather than just the tangible assets you are creating. Both are important - one to increase the emotional balance sheet and the other our net balance sheet (our assets minus our liabilities, such as mortgages and debts).

Fear of success is an interesting fear! It is often the fear of not being able to handle the responsibilities that come with said success. We do a great job, therefore, of staying in the same money beliefs or money situations with our savings balances because we fear the success of money flowing to us with ease.

For most of us, these fears stem from childhood. In childhood, the situations that create the fear are magnified. Have you ever noticed that whenever you think back to a time in childhood when you felt embarrassed or scared, you can now see how much less significant the event was. As adults, we apply more logic to the situation. For that child, though, the brain has stored that experience and catalogued it as a threat. It does not want us to re-experience that pain and keeps us stuck in patterns of limitations.

Activity: *My limiting fears*

To begin this exercise, write down all the types of fear of failure or fear of success scenarios that you experienced growing up. The younger you were, the better.

Now write down all the types of fear of failure or fear of success scenarios that you worry about if you were to fulfil some of your desires.

For each new experience you want to create, write down how you would react to it coming from a place of expansive possibilities.

Then ask yourself, if I had already done this one thing and I stepped beyond the fear, what would be possible for me?

The next step, now that we have acknowledged the fears, is to bring this future into today. In order to see clearly what our future self desires, we need to expand our mental time horizons so that our future self is no longer a stranger but an extension of our current self. We need to move our future self desires to the present day ... (OMG how exciting!)

Take a moment to think about what you'll be doing 10 years prior to that 90th birthday celebration. Follow the same process: what do you see? Who is with you?

Do the same for 20 years prior to that 90th birthday.

Then 30 years.

Keep going until you get back to 12 months ahead of *now*.

If you could choose three of your biggest desires to have absolute focus on, what would they be? Let's call these your three rocks. Why rocks? Rocks are analogous to the big, important things in your life that give it meaning: family, partner, health, goals and dreams. If you take actual physical rocks and put them in a glass jar, you'll find that there's space left over for smaller objects like pebbles, sand and water. The pebbles represent other things that give our lives meaning – our career, our home, our friendships. The sand and water represent the smaller things that aren't as significant, but tend to fill our time up quickly - things like watching TV, scrolling social media, etc. By focusing on the three big rocks first, you're still able to fit many of these other things in. However, if you try to do it in reverse order, the big things will get left out.

Why three? Well ... proponents of the *Rule of Three* state that things are more engaging, satisfying and more effectively presented when in threes, for example: *Ready, Steady, Go; The Good, the Bad and the Ugly; The Three Little Pigs; The Three Musketeers! Deserve, Create, Grow.*

Activity: *My three future self big rocks are:*

Now break these rocks down into small steps of action. I like to batch mine into quarterly rocks, then monthly, then weekly.

What do you need to do today to make some of these things possible? Perhaps you imagined yourself hosting retreats for young mothers or creating a foundation to help women in abusive relationships ... perhaps you have helped your local community to reduce their use of plastic.

What is the world calling for you?

CHAPTER 52
RESISTANCE

I bet at this point in the book you are feeling some resistance - resistance to success. Am I right? You have likely set yourself goals or intentions in the past that you are no further forward on, those deep and meaningful life desires. You are likely no further forward with taking actions on these because of one thing. Resistance. How do you know if this is present for you? You will feel it internally, that breathlessness or pang of ickiness in your stomach. Resistance is fuelled by fear. If we can master fear we can master resistance. All this feeling is, is self-sabotage. It can come from yourself and your own limitations or from other people. Have you ever experienced this? You start to do something truly remarkable for yourself and somebody tells you that you are not capable or worthy. Your success becomes a reproach to their own sense of self because it triggers their own resistance. Perhaps you have experienced this from a family member or a 'friend'. You do know that this is all about their own resistance, not yours, don't you? It's back to those borrowed beliefs again but this time it manifests itself in borrowed resistance. Our own resistance often shows itself in procrastination. We put things off. We tell ourselves we will do it another day. *I will stop overspending next month. I will start writing that book next year. I will take that extra time for myself next week.* We literally put things off right up until the very moment that it is too late. We fill our time being busy - busy procrastinating and resisting the one thing that will move us closer to our vision and purpose. Sometimes procrastination can be positive. There's often a hidden message inside the emotion. The challenge comes when we fall into victim mode and blame ourselves or others for the lack of action in our lives.

There are two things certain in life. Death and taxes. Don't let resistance stop you from achieving something you were put on this earth to fulfil. We all have a sense of our purpose, often guided by intuition.

Let me share what happened when I stopped resisting ...

Catherine's story: *Catherine*

On 1st January 2021 I was out walking with my family in the fields around the village where we lived at that time. Every New Year's Day we have a conversation about our intentions for the year ahead - what we've enjoyed about the last 12 months, and what we want to create more of for the year ahead. It is our 'moments that matter' conversation, something we've got into the habit of doing. We walk and talk and then we come home and we all write down three things that matter to us for the year ahead. We put them in a jar labelled 'The Morgans' 2021 Moments That Matter' and we open the jar again on 31st December. This year, as we were walking across the cold, frosty fields, I shared with my husband that I felt a continued calling to be close to the water. The water gives me a feeling of space, calm and serenity. I feel safe by the water. Then, during a call with one of my coaches, Jo, who I'd been working with for the previous year, she told me - before I said anything - that this year she could see me living in Jersey. So, I pinned a photo up on my office wall of Jersey with the word *spaciousness*. I'd been delaying our kitchen renovations for months and couldn't understand why, or what was stopping me, and the following week I had a call with a branding expert Nicole. Whilst helping me summarise my vision statement she said: 'The word that is coming up for me here, Catherine, is spaciousness' ... and I started to imagine my life by the sea. Less than eight weeks later my husband had a job offer for us to return to live in Jersey in the Channel Islands. We had manifested this! It was the first time I'd really experienced the law of attraction and manifestation for myself. I couldn't believe it. Whether it was manifestation or actually just facing the resistance we often feel to making big moves like this, time will tell!

As I write this book I am living in Jersey and have experienced an extraordinary shift since moving here. I can only describe this shift as a spiritual awakening. I was driving back from Pilates one night along the seafront. It was dusk and the sky was so beautiful against the backdrop of the crashing waves against the rocks that I stopped the car and parked up. I sat listening to the waves and smelling the salty air for about 20 minutes before heading back up the hill towards home. Within seconds of pulling away I had a huge panic attack. The sea was literally calling me back. I spun my car around in the middle of the road and drove back towards the sea. As I sat, staring out at what felt like the edge of the earth, I wondered what had just happened and suddenly realised what it was. The spaciousness of the sea was calling me closer to my twin brother in Australia. The sea had called me back to be with him. I burst into tears as it became clear why I had wanted to move back to Jersey. Each morning as I walk my dog up on the heath, I feel so connected to him, despite the distance and the time since we last spoke.

So - whatever your dreams and desires, this is your time to be intentional. Make it happen! Because you *deserve* to *grow*.

CHAPTER 53
FINANCIAL REGRETS

A little word on financial regret ...

When we begin to look at our future, this small but mighty emotion tends to pop up like a sore thumb. We all make money mistakes. Period. Then we compound and magnify these regrets by not talking about them.

You are not alone if your pension pots are non-existent.

You are not alone if you don't have a financial security fund.

You are not alone if you have debts (money already spent!)

You are not alone if you have money shame.

I want you to *own* your regrets, not ignore or bury them. If we acknowledge them we can let them go!

Speak your financial regrets. Heal your financial wounds. Release the shame that you have been carrying.

A financial company in the UK, *Hargreaves Lansdown*[1], conducted some research and concluded that one in five people (20%) regrets leaving it too late to build a rainy day savings pot, while a similar proportion (19%) wish they had started saving earlier for retirement.

So you are not alone!

An Australian nurse, Bronnie Ware, spent several years working in palliative care with patients in the last 12 weeks of their lives. She recorded their dying epiphanies in a blog called *Inspiration and Chai*, which she then put into a book called *The Top Five Regrets of the Dying*.[2]

Here are the top five regrets of the dying, as witnessed by Ware:

1. I wish I'd had the courage to live a life true to myself, not the life others expected of me.

'This was the most common regret of all. When people realise that their life is almost over and look back clearly on it, it is easy to see how many dreams have gone unfulfilled. Most people had not honoured even a half of their dreams and had to die knowing that it was due to choices they had made, or not made. Health brings a freedom very few realise, until they no longer have it.'

2. I wish I hadn't worked so hard.

'This came from every male patient that I nursed. They missed their children's youth and their partner's companionship. Women also spoke of this regret, but as most were from an older generation, many of the female patients had not been breadwinners. All of the men I nursed deeply regretted spending so much of their lives on the treadmill of a work existence.'

3. I wish I'd had the courage to express my feelings.

'Many people suppressed their feelings in order to keep peace with others. As a result, they settled for a mediocre existence and never became who they were truly capable of becoming. Many developed illnesses relating to the bitterness and resentment they carried as a result.'

4. I wish I had stayed in touch with my friends.

'Often they would not truly realise the full benefits of old friends until their dying weeks and it was not always possible to track them down. Many had become so caught up in their own lives that they had let golden friendships slip

by over the years. There were many deep regrets about not giving friendships the time and effort that they deserved. Everyone misses their friends when they are dying.'

5. I wish that I had let myself be happier.

'This is a surprisingly common one. Many did not realise until the end that happiness is a choice. They had stayed stuck in old patterns and habits. The so-called 'comfort' of familiarity overflowed into their emotions, as well as their physical lives. Fear of change had them pretending to others, and to themselves, that they were content, when deep within, they longed to laugh properly and have silliness in their life again'.

So whilst this may sound dramatic, think about what is *really* important to you in your life. Ask yourself, is there anything that you may regret later.

———

Activity: *Think about these questions:*

What may I regret later on if it's not one of my three focus areas (rocks)?

What would I do if I created time for myself rather than working?

What actions or behaviours do I need to honour as non-negotiable?

What friends do I value the most and how can I spend more time with them?

What am I doing just because others expect it of me?

———

'I don't want to make money. I just want to be wonderful.'

— **MARILYN MONROE**

The Feeling and Doing Money Wheel

We often feel pulled in so many different directions when it comes to growing wealth. How we feel about the following often distracts us from building a strong financial future:

Receiving money (deserving)

Holding on to money (creating)

Giving money (growing)

Being incongruent in just one of these areas can take up so much of our energy that we either make enough money and can't keep hold of it, hold on to too much and don't take enough risks (we hoard cash only for inflation to erode its buying power) or give it all way to others' needs whilst sacrificing our own.

We might also feel overwhelmed by the 'stuff' we have to do around these areas. We just think 'Aah … I'll sort it out another day.' Am I right?!

Having explored the emotional side in the *Deserve* section of this book, I want to focus here on some practical steps for you.

In order to get into balance and feel congruent with money, explore which areas of your money behaviour need your attention. Start by drawing a *Money Wheel*.

Activity: *5 Steps to completing your 'Feeling and Doing Money Wheel'*

I have given some suggested areas to explore (the headings on the rim of the wheel) but you may wish to label these yourself with areas that are applicable to you.

Grab two coloured pens and look at each spoke of the wheel. Rate with one coloured dot on a scale of 1-10 how you *feel* currently. Then rate it again in a different colour according to how much time and attention you're giving to that area - how you are *doing*. Zero = you are ignoring it. 10 = you are giving it maximum attention and you feel safe and fulfilled in this area.

Once you have marked them with a small dot, join the *feeling* dots together in one colour and the *doing* dots in another to form two odd shapes.

Stand back and observe. What do you notice? Are you doing something well only when you feel good about it? Are you ignoring something that you feel bad about? What patterns of behaviour do you see?

Identify which of the areas need your attention the most. Which of these do you feel most motivated to change? The goal is not to score 10/10 in each area as money is never linear, so what small steps of action are required for you to move from the number you are currently on to the next number? What small step can you take now?

Identify who can help you with this. Repeat this sentence out loud: 'WHO can help me with my next step?' This is the time to reach out to a financial coach or a financial planner/adviser for help. Or perhaps this is the time to have a money date with your partner so that you can decide who is going to take responsibility for the next steps.

Adopting the *Who not How* attitude will help you reach your next financial milestone much faster.

In the centre of your wheel is your heart and brain. 90% of our decisions about money are based on how we feel rather than what we think we should do. Recognise where you are now. This is all about being *consciously aware* in order to feel *and* do better.

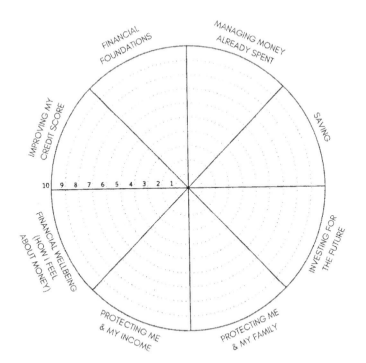

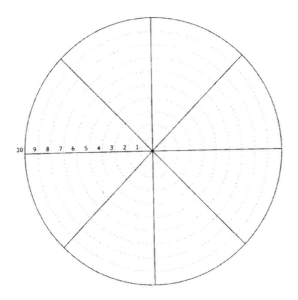

You can then devote the necessary time, energy and attention to all areas of the wheel. You can download a copy of the wheel at www.itsnotaboutthemoney.com/tools.

CHAPTER 54
LAW OF SUBTRACTION

I'd like to share a concept that's been written about by Matthew E. May in his book *The Laws of Subtraction*.[1]

Matthew states that we live in a world of excess, a world of content - social media, blogs, videos, podcasts, memberships, mastermind courses, programmes - *excess* everything. Excess content. *The Laws of Subtraction* is about the art of removing anything that is excessive, confusing, wasteful, complicated. And here's the thing: it's mind blowing. There are three critical choices inherent to every decision we make in our life, in our business, in our finances, with our families - and those three critical things are:

1. What to pursue
2. What to leave
3. What to do

The opposites of those are the things that we rarely pay attention to. For example, in thinking about what to pursue, we rarely think about what to ignore. We might think: *I need to be attracting more clients, making more money, creating more time, writing more blogs, doing more Facebook Lives. I need to be creating more money.* But if, for example, we scrolled less on our phones, how much more time and wealth could we create?

What to leave in vs what to leave out

What could you do without right now? What have you always had but don't need anymore? What saps your finances? Your time? Energy? Resources? With regard to your direct debits and subscriptions, what do you need and what do you not need? What can you remove? What can you subtract? What can you minimise? What is complicated in your life right now that you could just delete from it? Occasionally, doing *something* isn't better than doing *nothing*. Sometimes when you wake up in the morning feeling overwhelmed, one of the best things you can do for yourself is nothing.

And if you feel you *do* have to deal with the overwhelm, get it out of your head and onto some paper. Dance to some music. Have a glass of wine. Have a walk in nature. Just get everything *out* and you'll be in a much better position to deal with anything.

What to do vs what not to do

Rather than overwhelming yourself with a huge list of the things you need to do right now, think about what you *don't* need to do. Create some good boundaries - around your energy, your time, your relationships. Some of you might even be questioning your friendships right now – which of your friends are there for you at the moment? Which are not? This kind of thinking gets you to re-evaluate lots of things.

Matthew E. May says that success is about one key skill - subtracting rather than adding. How might that apply to you in your life right now?

CHAPTER 55

CREATING BOUNDARIES

We often have a challenging relationship with money because we are over-dominate in giving, receiving, saving or spending. You might be really strong on what your mission, your purpose, is, but you won't achieve it without strong boundaries. If your inbox is constantly full, you could end up in a position where you're so overwhelmed with everything coming your way that your wellbeing suffers.

1. Make self-care a priority.

It doesn't have to be huge. Read your book or spend 15 minutes a day listening to a meditation track - anything that is about you and not about those incoming notifications.

2. Create boundaries.

What are your boundaries? When is the point that when your boundary is crossed you feel bad, uncomfortable or depleted? If you don't like working in the evening because your energy levels are low, the evening is your boundary. What one thing may people not know that you need? Space? Time? Not to work in the evenings? Recognise and communicate what your boundaries are, or nobody will know.

3. The alternative to Yes or No.

Remember that you don't have to give either a yes or a no answer to requests made of you. You also have the option of saying *not right now*.

4. Learn to let go.

Is something you're doing just not working? Let it go. Let go of bad relationships. Let go of negative people in your life. If people are putting negative things on your social media, for example, just block them and move on. You don't have time to take in that negative energy.

5. Listen to your intuition.

You know those times when you meet someone and that nugget of intuition inside you says 'I'm not quite sure'? This is your own internal alarm system, your red flag - if that red flag is going off, it usually means you need to listen.

If you're trying to make a decision about something and it doesn't feel quite right then either say no or put it on the *maybe in the future* pile. Listen to your intuition. In most situations, your intuition is correct.

6. Notice what drains you.

Again this is a little bit intuitive, but if you can identify what is draining you and focus on improving that area, it can help with creating really strong boundaries and avoiding overwhelm.

Notice what activities you're doing, what tasks you're performing, what relationships you have. Life is too short to be drained by people, jobs, activities, things that are taking us off track.

CHAPTER 56
GRATITUDE

Neuroscience tells us that gratitude and happiness register almost identically in the brain. In gratitude, everything is enough. It is an *abundance*, *more than enough* state of being. It has the ability to transform *not enoughness* to *more than enoughness* and deep fulfilment.

Practising gratitude can also assist with one of the biggest human fears linked to poor financial decisions - the fear of missing out (FOMO). When we are fearful of missing out, we focus on what we don't have rather than gratitude for what we do have. The solution for FOMO is to practise being truly present, noticing everything and everyone around us. These small details contribute to the moments that make up the here and now and help us to feel pure gratitude for what we have rather than what we don't have.

On a daily basis, reflecting on what you're grateful for that day is so empowering. I have a gratitude diary next to my bed. I don't write in it every night. Sometimes I do it at night, sometimes in the morning. Being grateful for those little things is useful when we're not feeling particularly positive. Don't get me wrong ... I have days and times where I just feel emotional, where I need to go and cry. And I think we need to do that, to recognise that actually being sad and having a good cry is sometimes all we need to do. Or dancing in the kitchen. Otherwise, we store it in our body, and you know now what kind of impact that can have on your wellbeing.

Every day, perhaps whilst brushing your teeth, say something to yourself that helps you to feel grateful for what you've achieved in your business or personal life that day. As women, we define ourselves and our self-worth through our relationships. Many men define their self-worth through their work. It's the hunter-gatherer in them. So - by practising more gratitude and self-love, the more you will be open to receive ... more clients, more money. And by focusing on both, long-term, consistent results will follow.

CHAPTER 57
STEP INTO GRATITUDE - THE HOW

 'A flower does not think of competing with the flower next to it, it just blooms.'

— **ZEN SHIN**

When we are able to truly express gratitude, we step into a state of appreciation. We stop complaining. How many times have you, honestly, complained that you don't have enough money? That you perhaps feel jealous of someone else for their success? How many times have you felt triggered by somebody else's success? I have definitely experienced this and really, what does it achieve other than reinforce limiting beliefs? The less we judge, the more we appreciate. 'But how do I stop doing this?' I hear you ask. Well, by stepping into a state of appreciation, we step into a state of desiring and attracting more as if it has already happened. We begin thinking and behaving like that wealthy woman. We begin taking responsibility with money to create an exceptional life. Are you ready for this? If you are, write this sentence down (even if you just write it inside this page): *It is safe for me to take responsibility with money.*

Yay! You're now ready to receive.

You may have heard of the law of attraction and perhaps you feel a little sceptical. *Do I just close my eyes and wish there was more money in my bank account?* The law of attraction is centred on how we create the relationships, situations and material things that come into our lives as a direct consequence of the way we think and the unconscious beliefs that underpin that. We 'manifest' them by focusing on them, visualising them becoming true and directing our energy towards them through the actions we take. Focusing our energy and attention towards something can make it happen. This may sound 'woo woo' but it's all about our focus and what distracts us from this focus, what replenishes our energy and what drains us. The difference between making something happen or not is the action over the intention. It needs to be purposeful, directed and in alignment. *Alignment* is that sweet spot between the heart and the mind, a place where you feel in congruence with your goals and your life's purpose. Science is proving that there is a deep brain-body connection and when we tune in and listen to this, we feel in alignment. We are primed for success.

What happens when we are not in alignment? *Cognitive dissonance!* (see the *Create* section) These exercises, therefore, will support your physical as well as your financial wellbeing.

In order for you to be primed for success, I'm introducing you to two exercises - the *Monthly Money Date* and the *Weekly Reflection*.

CHAPTER 58

THE MONTHLY MONEY DATE

A money date is one of the most important dates in your diary and one of the most important commitments you can have with yourself. A money date is a specific time you commit in your diary for your relationship with money. For me it is not always so much about the practical steps but more so about awareness and intention - both of which embody the key themes of the first two sections of this book. It's all about connecting with money with complete clarity, knowing where you are and where you're going, and beginning to very gently nurture the next steps for creating the future you desire.

Setting the scene

A money date can be planned or spontaneous. I believe that it should be both - that you have a fixed day and time in your diary for your money date and that you should also be prepared to go with the flow.

If you wake up one day feeling that you really want to get to understand your numbers or have a look at where you're going in your business, or even take a look at some of those disempowering beliefs you're holding on to, then just go with the flow. Don't wait for that date to arrive. Feeling high on energy creates opportunity for taking some action. Equally, if you set a date with yourself and when it comes you're just not feeling it, don't worry. Reschedule that date, allowing yourself some spontaneity in between. And think about time. For me, Sunday is a great day for a money date. I wake up, grab a cup of tea and bring it back to bed. I have my own candle range with a scent designed to reinvigorate and energize the mind and body, which I find really helps. I draw open my curtains slightly so I've got a little light in the room ... 'peace' for me is lowering the lights. For you, it might be putting on some energizing music and busting it out. What will get *you* in the mood for facing some of those challenges and disempowering beliefs? Choose an environment conducive to creativity, honesty and allowing yourself to open up to some of the challenges for you around money right now. And make that environment as clutter-free and calm as possible. I have my notepads and my journal and I use that opportunity to really reflect on where I am and where I want to be, and I start setting intentions.

It should be fun, not a serious, boring task.

Trying to find an hour a month for your money date might be a challenge. However, finding 15 minutes a week is 100% doable for most people, most weeks. You can even do it lying on a sunbed. If you choose a monthly money date, you may wish to consider allowing a bit more time.

Prepare the body - a little science lesson

If you begin to feel some resistance to this exercise, you'll likely feel it first in the body ... your hands, throat, head, stomach. We want the nervous system to feel safe first before we work on the action steps, so we need to slow it down and help it feel regulated. The part of the body that deals with this is the vagus nerve. The vagus nerve is your body's superpower and it's used to counteract the flight/fight response. If you feel unsafe, stressed, fearful about looking at money, regulation of your vagus nerve can result in a calmer, more compassionate, clearer response. Stimulation of the vagus nerve and focusing on a healthy vagal tone leads to emotional regulation, greater connection and even better physical health. Who knew one nerve could do so much! It is actually the longest cranial nerve in the body. Its name comes from the Latin *vagus*, for *wandering*, because it wanders throughout your body. The nervous system controls your organs and glands and is made up of two subsystems - the *sympathetic* and *parasympathetic*. The sympathetic nervous system prepares the body for stress-related activities and the parasympathetic nervous system is associated with returning the body to routine. Every time your brain perceives a threat, the sympathetic nervous system triggers the fight or flight response. The parasympathetic nervous system does the opposite - it calms you. It is activated when a danger is over, such as being pulled away from ongoing traffic while crossing the street.

There are some fun, easy ways to activate the parasympathetic nervous system. You can access this now by running your finger down the back of your neck. Give it a little massage! Drink a glass of ice cold water. While your body is busy adjusting to the coldness of the water, the sympathetic activity declines and the parasympathetic activity increases, bringing us back to a state of calmness. Singing and humming can activate these muscles and stimulate the vagus nerve, too. As if we needed an excuse to stick on our favourite piece of music and have a good old sing! Create a playlist for yourself and name it your *PS Money date* (PS = parasympathetic) album.

Also, any type of deep, slow, diaphragmatic breathing will stimulate your vagus nerve and activate your parasympathetic nervous system.

Visualise filling up the lower part of your lungs just above your belly button like a balloon ... and then exhaling slowly, breathing in through the nose and out through the mouth.

Breath work is one of the most effective trauma tools that I've used on my healing journey. Our breath changes with our emotions. Most cultures globally have always had an understanding of the power of the breath as a healing tool. This is why most schools of meditation use the breath to help guide us inward. Breath work allows us to take in more oxygen, which can alter and improve gland function and the endocrine system. Increased oxygen also allows us to massage our organs and detox our bodies.

As we detox our bodies, we also begin to release the thoughts, memories or beliefs we were holding onto and start to process and integrate these, which helps us heal trauma and our nervous system.

Chanting whilst meditating is effective for stimulating the vagal nerve. This reminds me of childhood when my twin brother and I would go to the local Buddhist temple and chant 'nam myoho renge kyo'. Little did I know that the 10-year-old version of me had actually just experienced a vagal tone stimulation practice.

An interesting study was performed by the *International Journal of Yoga*[1] in 2011, where *OM* chanting was compared with a rest state to determine if chanting is more stimulatory to the vagus nerve. The study found that the chanting was more effective.

I want you to create a 'disempowering beliefs' page on a piece of paper. Write down all of those little inner critic messages that are coming through, the ones in which you're telling yourself you're not worthy or you're not capable. Capture those in a single place. Think about how many of your beliefs have come from your family, how many are borrowed beliefs. When we don't feel worthy, we begin to develop patterns that prevent us from having the money we want and deserve. When we feel that we aren't good enough with money, we also feel fear that we won't have enough. So by getting rid of those disempowering, borrowed beliefs, saying 'I *am* good enough, I'm taking this time for myself. I am good enough' the fear of not having enough will begin to dissipate. We'll be coming from a place of empowerment. The greatest financial obstacle we face is our lack of awareness of the mind, the body, the spirit and their connections to our bank account. Something almost none of us have ever been taught. Instead, we unknowingly hold on to these beliefs as our truth, thus reducing the possibility that the money we want and need can flow to us.

Essentially, it's just energy. We all wake up with the same amount of energy in the morning. Closing ourselves off to opportunities because of these disempowering beliefs closes off that energy. As soon as we begin to change our language, our body will reflect that new belief. Think about what beliefs you may be holding on to and make sure that you note those down on your disempowering beliefs page.

Assess where your emotions are right now, rating them on a scale from 1-10, with 10 being your highest stress level. Just before a money date, anything over a 7 means reschedule! You should be in a positive frame of mind, otherwise it will be a disempowering exercise. You may find instead that it's a good opportunity to focus on those disempowering beliefs.

Anything between a 1 and 7 is OK ... you'll have your *disempowering beliefs* page with you, which will give you an opportunity to park anything on there that is holding you back.

We've talked about preparation of the body and the mind, timing and ambience. You should also prepare your focus.

Prepare your focus

Review your financial intentions, the destination of your boat, the steps you've set to move you closer to where you want to be, how you'll feel when you get there. You're gently stretching your financial comfort zone here. Be honest with yourself. Focus on the results you will create. Always keep the end in mind.

Prepare your behaviours

As many of you know, I'm a big believer in something called behavioural finance, which looks at the psychological reasons why we don't do certain things around money. Think about creating habit changes and also maintaining things that are working in your favour.

For example, what have you been avoiding for too long? Tracking your numbers? Going VAT registered? Setting up a Facebook group? Have you been avoiding showing up on camera? Have you been avoiding that awkward conversation with your boss? Have you been avoiding opportunities for creating your own business? Or even a side hustle? Have you avoided creating a website because you can't get past the technical bits? Journal for a few minutes around what you could do to move one step closer towards getting these things done.

Sticking to your intentions will bring about new behaviours. Having knowledge of your numbers, tracking money coming in and going out, will give you the confidence to build that emergency fund or begin investing. What kinds of behavioural changes might you begin to see in this particular step?

Final steps - Schedule and Celebrate

Schedule your future money dates. Choose a future date to review your progress from this meeting with yourself.

Celebrate and review. Take the time to celebrate, if only to tell yourself 'Well done'. It might be that you decide to take yourself off for a nice hot bubble bath or purchase a new candle, or go out for a walk in nature. It doesn't have to be big, but it's good to reward the positive behaviours and to review what went well last month, what didn't go quite so well and what you'd do differently next time. Would you need to schedule a bit more time in your diary? Do you need to reach out for some support from somebody else? Should you read a book or listen to a podcast on a particular subject?

CHAPTER 59

PREVENTION

WHAT PREVENTS YOU FROM REACHING YOUR GOALS (LOSS AVERSION)

Another money behaviour I see is setting goals and not implementing them, setting goals and not reaching them, or setting goals and being so overwhelmed by them that nothing happens and nothing takes place. This is called *loss aversion*.

Imagine you are on your way to work, walking rather than driving or commuting. It's a beautiful day, the sun is shining and you can hear the birds singing. You're looking down at the path, seeing beautiful spring flowers starting to blossom and you spot out of the corner of your eye a £20 note. You pick it up and look around. You're alone so you think 'What am I going to do with this? I'm going to put it in my pocket'. For a moment you feel incredible joy that you've been lucky enough to have found this money. Perhaps even some shame around finding money that does not belong to you (go back to the *Deserve* section!)

You roll it up, pop it in your back pocket and continue your walk to work. You're in a great mood and you're now thinking about what to spend it on. There's a shop in the village with a jumper in the window that you've had your eye on for some time, and you notice that it's just gone into the sale. With this £20 in your back pocket you walk into the shop, take the jumper off the rail and to the cashier, handing it over with a little smile, thinking 'I've just found this £20 note and now I'm going to buy this jumper for myself'. Maybe you haven't treated yourself for a while, maybe you don't like to spend money on yourself because you feel guilty or you feel some shame. It's fine to spend money on others but not on yourself, so you're overjoyed to be able to do this. You reach into your back pocket for the £20 note and it's not there. Did you put it in the other pocket? It's not there, either. Maybe you put it in your bag. But no. The £20 note has disappeared.

How do you feel? The likelihood is you're feeling embarrassed, maybe disappointed, maybe absolute disbelief, wondering where on earth this £20 has gone.

What is loss aversion?

There has been a lot of research into loss aversion, suggesting that the pain of loss is twice as much as the joy we get from a gain. The pleasure you experienced from finding that £20 is half the pain you feel at the loss of it.

I am writing this during the summer of 2021. We are going through serious economic struggles as a result of the worldwide outbreak of the Coronavirus. Everyone is on tenterhooks: what's happening to the markets? What about my investments? Should I even be investing right now? There is a lot of uncertainty about what will happen. This loss aversion bias is a human bias, and very relevant right now.

How to conquer loss aversion

Interestingly, when we set goals or intentions for ourselves, they usually centre around a positive outcome: *if I save this amount of money I can go on a wonderful holiday*, or *if I pay down the rest of this debt I can be debt-free and then it won't ever happen again*.

What would happen if you turned this on its head, so rather than setting goals and focusing on the positive outcomes you thought about the opportunity lost? What would be the consequences if you don't take action or achieve that goal?

For example: 'I want to be debt free in six months': you've worked out that you can do it, and you know it's going to reduce your financial stress. What would happen if you don't focus on achieving this, if you don't put all your efforts into making this happen? What's the cost to you of that missed opportunity?

Many of you, like me, will be big fans of creating vision boards. I even do this in my Starling Bank app and have pictures behind my pots which really encourages me. But what about doing an anti-vision board?! What would your life look like if you didn't take action?

I wanted to plant that seed here. I'm not suggesting you focus on the pain, but think about the missed opportunities of not reaching those goals and intentions. Instead of focusing on the pleasurable outcome, what would happen if you changed the focus?

CHAPTER 60
THE WEEKLY REFLECTION

E very Sunday I sit down with a piece of paper and split it into four: *Wins, Challenges, Lessons, Focus*. There is a template you can download for this for you over at;

www.itsnotaboutthemoney.com/tools

MY WINS	MY CHALLENGES
LESSONS	FOCUS

WEEKLY *reflection*

First, I look at what I have achieved that week - **my wins**: e.g. reaching my business targets, finishing a book or walking 10,000 steps a day (I still struggle with that one!) When thinking about achievements, it's often the little things that make the biggest difference. Then I think about the **challenges**, the things that have got in my way. These could be myself, others or frustrations outside my control. These challenges often turn into reflections. I then consider the **lessons** I've learned - about myself, the world, my family, my health, my values. There will always be an opportunity to learn. I love collecting all of these lessons up at the end of the year. I should perhaps publish these one day!

Finally, I identify my **focus** for the week ahead. What is *your* focus? It should always link to your vision - anything else is just a distraction. Part of your vision may be to make a certain amount of money in your business. More income enables you to have more impact in the world. Let me say that again: ***more income enables you to have more impact in the world.*** Did I just touch on a money block? Yes, more money enables you to create more impact. More money often leads to more time and more time leads to more energy to help more people. One of my money narratives was 'It is safe for me to make more money'. You can borrow that one if you like!

Test your focus areas by questioning your commitment using the *Would* and *Would not* questions.

1. What *wouldn't* happen if I *did* create more focus in this area?
2. What *would* happen if I *did* create more focus in this area?
3. What *wouldn't* happen if I *didn't* create more focus in this area?
4. What *would* happen if I *didn't* create more focus in this area?

This is going to be your master plan! One that you will refer back to weekly to begin with. We don't do this very often - we usually focus on the negative, the 'not enough'.

Comparisonitis is evil!

Whenever I ask what financial security looks like the typical response is five or ten grand a month. Why? Is that what everybody else seems to be doing? In truth, you might only need to earn half or a quarter of that. We suffer from *comparisonitis* - doing what others are doing and not staying in our own lane. I wish I hadn't compared myself with others and hankered so much after the equivalent of the *Instagram* life, but I know it's human nature to compare and contrast. If you find yourself doing that, get back in your own lane. Compare yourself only to where *you* were yesterday, where *you've* come from - and then look forward to where you want to be. Focus on what's important to *you*. Take pride and be grateful for everything in your life. Think about what you value and create goals around those things. This is *your* path. If you see other people doing amazing things, that's brilliant ... let them inspire you, not lead you into a different direction.

But first, we are going to make you feel good. Feeling good helps you to think positively and move from disempowered to self-empowered. Are you ready? Let's go.

CHAPTER 61

YOUR FINANCIAL COMFORT BOX

G rab a box - any kind - and place in it five items that make you feel good through each one of your senses: sight, sound, smell, touch, taste.

Sight - You could pop your money narrative cards in here so that you can spend a few moments reading these out to yourself.

Sound - I often play music when I am having a money date with myself. You could create a music playlist for when you are about to open up your bank statements.

Smell - Perhaps you'll choose a luxurious candle whose scent reminds you of something on your vision board ... perhaps a salt candle smelling of the sea, where you envisage yourself living in the future.

Touch - How about putting in a silk scarf or warm blanket or perhaps a smooth crystal that represents strength and abundance? People often say to allow a crystal to choose you but here are a few to get started: green jade has been used in Chinese history to attract wealth and harmony; clear quartz can help you declutter and clarify your intention; malachite is a stunning emerald-hued stone that will impart the strength and courage to transform any fears or doubts in regards to money; citrine is one of the most powerful stones for manifestation as it will help you bring your financial goals to life as well as enhance your confidence and abundance. I rub the crystal between my hands before I begin, say my money mantra out loud and focus on my intention.

Taste - As if we need any excuse to have something delicious! Buy yourself a bar of luxury chocolate or your favourite shortbread biscuits or grab some fruit from the fridge. Or perhaps pop some herbal tea bags in there and make yourself a lovely brew. I use *Fortnum and Mason* tea bags because they give me a sense of luxury and remind me that I deserve these small upgrades. We want your body to feel good and be nurtured. This is particularly important if money makes you feel anxious.

Now - very, very gently begin to stretch your boundaries. Focus on where you're at right now. Focus on a strong intention. Close your eyes and think about what deserves your focus in the here and now. Step into Wealth® by celebrating wealth as if it is already available for you. You might imagine yourself in that dream home by the sea every time you open that box. Each time you imagine your dreams as if they are already happening, you are giving the world a signal that you deserve this. That you are ready for this. It is your time.

CHAPTER 62
YOUR FINANCIAL CLOSET PLAN

 'When you visualize, then you materialize.'

— **DENIS WAITLEY**

O nce we are able to feel good about money, we often need some help to create some order around it. I want you to create a *financial closet plan*. 'Closet' is a perfect analogy: when buying clothes we aim for a balance of well-fitted underwear, good staple basics and then some fun accessories to jazz up our look. In organising your money there is no cookie cutter approach - just as our closets would not look the same, neither would our financial systems. We each have our unique style.

CHAPTER 63

YOUR TWO FINANCIAL CLOSET PLANS

CAPSULE AND ULTIMATE

The *Capsule Financial Plan* is a capsule wardrobe with all the key, basic pieces in place. Once you have your basic wardrobe you can invest in some high quality items or trends - a range of shoes, a range of colour accessories, a range of shapes that complement each other - your *Ultimate Financial Plan*. You must be able to visualise each plan as you design it so that each becomes your reality.

Activity: *The Capsule Financial Plan*

Take a piece of paper and draw out five columns. Think of them as shelves in your closet. Head up those columns as follows:

1) *Savings and Bank Balances* - list all your bank and savings balances. Do this exercise separately for your business accounts and personal accounts.

2) *Money Already Spent* (aka *debt*) - as you know by now, we have good debts and bad debts. Do not think about the

negative implications of decisions you've made in the past. We're in the here and now. This is money you've already spent for whatever reason. If you need to go and look at your credit card apps, your statement, or make a phone call to your provider for an up-to-date balance, do it. If you want to include student loans in there too, cool. You can put those under that column as well as any unsecured loans you may have. Just don't include your mortgage - we'll come to that separately.

3) *My future self* - estimate the current worth of your investment and pensions. If you get to this column and have no idea what they are worth or even where all your pensions are, that's fine. Your column may have nothing in it, and that's totally fine.

Some of you will have final salary pensions - pensions gold dust - where a fixed level of income is guaranteed for when you retire. Don't include that for the purpose of this exercise.

4) *Possessions* - include everything with a monetary value: cars, computers, televisions, furniture, bicycles, motorbikes, art, jewellery, stamp collections. What is its rough value?

5) *House Value* - if you are a homeowner, get an approximate value from *RightMove* or *Zoopla*. If you're feeling super brave, find out what your mortgage balance is and deduct that from the house value. Gently bring some awareness to what you currently have. Include any additional properties you have.

Once these figures are in place, write at the bottom of the page: *I am grateful for* ... and complete the sentence.

Perhaps you're grateful for having a final salary pension, for owning a home or having some savings pots for the kids. Maybe you're grateful for having less *money already spent* than you had a year ago. Pick out something that stands out for you, that really resonates. This exercise brings clarity. Have you been worrying about money already spent whilst sitting in a house worth £200,000?

With this clarity, identify the basics that are missing from your capsule plan. Does it need a financial security fund? A consistent income stream? A *future self* pot? Are you missing a pot for your freezer, a will, protection of your income? Write these down with a date for when you plan to address them. Get it? Ad-dress? Told you this would be fun!

Karen's story: Karen came to me having been through a horrendous divorce from which she retained the matrimonial home. She was deeply fearful that, having never looked after the family finances, she would run out of money. Whilst doing the *Capsule Financial Plan* exercise, she realised she had over £33k of guaranteed pension income from previous pensions and that she was sitting on £450k of equity in her home, as well as an inherited jewellery collection worth over £60k. We mapped out her current and future income desires and built her a financial plan. She left feeling confident about her financial future. It was such a lightbulb moment for her as she had forgotten she owned her home outright. It released the fear of not having enough. Sometimes when we focus on the jar, we lose sight of what is inside it.

Enjoy this exercise ... gaining that helicopter view of your finances will help you to see the bigger picture. Once your basic capsule plan is complete, you can move on to the next stage.

Activity: *The Ultimate Financial Plan*

Look at your basic capsule plan and identify what you can upgrade. Yes - upgrade! Of course, this is really about upgrading your mindset. True wealth is all about mindset. When you become truly confident in what you can create, you will step into a *more than enough* or *abundance* mindset. This mindset enables you to *feel* wealthy. It enables you to step into money narratives like:

I am good with money.

Having more money gives me the opportunity to contribute to others and create powerful change and impact in the world.

I am enough and I have enough

In upgrading our lives we should work on one area at a time. We should train the brain, build up those money muscles! And it *can* start small.

Remember the *Fridge/Freezer/Larder* concept you met in the *Create* section? Start with your fridge, then move on to your larder and freezer pots.

Do you have a bank account that isn't rewarding you?

Do you have a savings account that could earn more interest?

Do you have a credit card you'd like to pay off?

Does your credit report need some TLC?

Does your mortgage rate need reviewing?

Does your financial security fund need topping up?

Do you have a basic investment account and want to upgrade and diversify the risk?

Could you download any apps to help you manage money?

Is it time to conquer that mountain of financial paperwork?

Could you be clearer on your *needs* versus your *wants*?

Identify your action plan for upgrading these areas. Use the *Financial Wheel of Life* from the *Create* section of the book to get some help.

When are you going to make this happen? Pick a date and then reward yourself once you have done it. Upgrading is hugely important from a mindset perspective, so celebrate that. Celebrate Wealth!

Once you have created your financial closet, the next step is to organise it!

CHAPTER 64
MY MONEY CLOSET ORGANISER

'Clutter is nothing more than postponed decisions.'

— **BARBARA HEMPHILL**

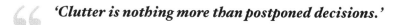

When I was training to be a personal stylist one of my favourite tasks was helping women declutter and organise their closets. I've always loved having my clothes, shoes and handbags in a tidy place. It helps me to see what I have, to declutter the chaos I've historically felt about clothes and my body confidence and also to identify the gaps. With clients, I'd start with a wardrobe declutter and once we'd identified the style, shapes and colours that suited them, we'd focus on what was missing. We'd lay outfits out on the bed and take photographs of items that went together, creating a *Pinterest* board or photo album on their phone so that the next time they were shopping they could see how items for sale went with what they already owned. The same can be done with money. We all want to be financially organised, but we rarely have the time to, ironically, organise! Financial documents and key pieces of information are all over the place - like our closets. I recommend that you store this information somewhere either online or in a book and that you update your money organiser once a year. In a worst case scenario it will save a lot of time and energy for others at a very emotional time. Get organised. Feel Good. Plan Well.

So - take stock, declutter, pair up, organise and store it where it can be accessed easily. You can do this in two ways:

Paper organising

Take all of your financial paperwork and create a simple folder with some key sections:

- Banking (fridge)
- Savings (larder)
- *Future me* pots (freezer - investments and pensions)
- Money already spent (loans, creditcards, mortgage statements)
- Personal possessions (e.g. jewellery)
- Children
- Insurances (home, car, health, pet, life, income)
- Health
- Tax
- Useful contacts list (accountant, solicitor, mortgage adviser, financial adviser, financial coach)
- Receipts and warranties
- Legal (will, Power of Attorney)

The thought of organising years of paperwork can be overwhelming but getting this done will bring clarity like never before. Make sure you keep financial paperwork relating to financial advice, disputes and tax information for seven years. Never store the original, sole copy of your will or the title deeds to your house in your home.

Digital organising

Digital paperwork can be accessed anywhere in the world. Once, when abroad, I needed to access some insurance documents and it was super easy.

Set up your categories in folders and subfolders on your computer, making sure you have regular back-ups scheduled and even protection software. You can create a password to the folders for added security. You can also consider using the cloud to store this data.

With this set-up, every time a new financial document comes in, scan it. I use *Adobe Scan* on my phone. I then convert the document to PDF and save it to the relevant folder.

Do the same for your business. I have a folder for each of my businesses, including sub-folders for accounts, VAT, payroll, etc. I create a folder for each year. At the end of the year I move it to an external hard drive and retrieve the information as and when I need it.

Now that your money is organised and has a home, it's time to think about ways to keep up the momentum. Let me introduce you to the *weekly money date*. This is my favourite part!

 'If you change the way you look at things, the things you look at will change.'

— WAYNE DYER

CHAPTER 65

NEEDS VERSUS WANTS

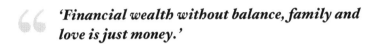

'Financial wealth without balance, family and love is just money.'

— ANDREAS SIMIC

When you have this weekly money date with yourself, think about what you need *and* what you want.

Some of you may be thinking you don't deserve to have wants. And some of you might find it difficult to split your needs from your wants. *Needs* are those things that are crucial for you to have in order to feel secure and safe with money. To establish your needs, reflect deeply on your relationship with money, and the stage of the wealth creation journey you are on.

We lose track of the importance of meeting our emotional needs and become distracted by our wants. When we don't really know what our hearts desire, our spending habits are redirected to 'stuff' that we buy in an attempt to try and fill this gap. Understanding your wants and how these differ from your needs is crucial to help you develop long-term healthy habits with money.

Both needs and wants are extrinsic. Simply put, *needs* are about 'fulfilling' yourself from the inside out and *wants* are about 'filling yourself up' from the outside in. Needs are about *being* and wants are about *having*.

The level of *beingness* allows you the *doingness* to get the *havingness*.

When we project a desire or wish for the future, inside the wish is something that is unfulfilled, something that we want more of. This is often emotional - we want to feel more content, secure, safe - so we align our spending to what we seek:

- What you spend is what you value
- What you save is what you seek
- What you give is what you desire

Moving from the unconscious to the conscious when spending money will ensure there is alignment between your actions and values.

A *need* can be tested. Try going without it for a month and see what happens. For *wants*, rather than asking the universe to make you rich, thank it for what you already have. In essence, you are thanking yourself for what you have already created and are already grateful for.

Give your wants something that is motivational, that evokes an emotional buy-in, otherwise your unconscious mind will prevent it from happening. It will feel unfamiliar and your brain will do everything it can to make you feel safe, avoiding the behaviour that holds too much uncertainty. The strength of your willingness is so important.

We have *enough* when all of our needs are met.

Fulfilling your needs does not mean having zero money to spend on the finer things in life. Far from it! Your spending plan should have some needs *and* wants. This is not about starving you of experiences or items you desire. It is about balancing your psychological and physical needs. Your needs will change over time, too. As you enter different life stages and life cycles, your needs will evolve, which is why we cannot judge what *we* need based on other people's needs!

Having the ability to feel deserving and then create a list of your needs is something I really want you to do. What comes up during the next exercise will be a light to the soul. Your deepest desires are often not met with money, but friendship, warmth, connection, community, love. Let's face it … many of us just want to *feel* love, *be* loved and *have* love.

Jane's story: When I started working with Jane she was a single mum of two boys, having divorced five years earlier. She ran her own health business and came to me because she was in a cycle of overspending. Whilst exploring her relationship with money she told me that her father abused her at the age of nine and that her mum was an unpresent mother. Her childhood was one of trauma and abandonment. Consequently, she believed that she didn't deserve to give to her own needs, so overspent money on her children by around £300 per month whilst her business was struggling.

Jane felt that by spending money on her children and giving them what she did not have as a child would make her feel loved. She gifted things in order to give and receive love. Becoming aware of this was hugely powerful as it meant she could begin working on ways to give herself that love and to explore other ways she could feel loved without going into debt.

This money pattern went back through the generations. Her father's father had done the same to him and her great-grandfather the same. In Mark Wolynn's book *It didn't start with you* he describes how these traumas 'can not only create a legacy of distress but also forge a legacy of strength and resilience that can be felt for generations to come'.

This work is so powerful. You are not just changing your own relationship with money. You are changing an inherited generational pattern for you and for every future generation. Imagine that.

CHAPTER 66
YOUR DESIRES LIST

In order to create a financial future enriched with enough money and time for the life we desire, we have to be clear on exactly what we desire. This is particularly important when thinking about our financial future. I don't know about you but the thought of 'retiring' on a park bench or to play golf (why does the media use these images to motivate us to invest?) fills me with dread! But creating a life where I can safeguard all the things that I love, that fill me with energy and fulfilment, is way more exciting ... and feels possible. This does not mean that we don't need practical financial planning in place to figure out how much to invest, but if we can see the path to wealth first, we are more likely to create it. And this all begins with desires.

Creating a 'desires list' is not something we're generally accustomed to doing. For many women, it can feel shameful to desire something for ourselves. Those money beliefs come out to play ... the *people pleaser*, the *enabler* narrative we looked at earlier in the book.

A desire is described as 'a strong feeling of wanting to have something or wishing for something to happen'. Notice the word *strong*? It has to be something your heart desires.

Let's set the scene ... light a candle, put some soft music on ... take a deep breath, place your hands on your heart and connect with your desires. What does your heart desire? Repeat these to yourself gently as you breathe in for three and out for six. Take the time to tell your nervous system that it is safe. And begin.

Take a piece of paper and draw out five columns with the following headings:

1. *Desires* 2. *Willingness* 3. *Havingness* 4. *Doingness* 5. *Time, Money, Energy*

DESIRES	WILLINGNESS	HAVINGNESS	DOINGNESS	TIME, MONEY, ENERGY

In column 1 write out 50 desires - things you seek: experiences, pleasures, places to visit, people to meet, communities to foster. You may find it hard to get to 50, but this is deliberate. Don't overthink this or the logical brain will take over. Ideally, your mind should be able to explore widely and wildly. What will support your wellbeing? What will give you intrinsic pleasure?

In column 2 rate on a scale of 1-10 how willing and motivated you are to create each one of these desires for yourself. Again, don't overthink it. Just add a number quickly to each desire.

In column 3 identify how much of this you already have. This could be an activity you do or a physical object you own.

In column 4 write the small steps you can take to make this happen.

In column 5 add figures for how much money, energy and time you need to allocate to this. For example, let's say you desire more time to travel and you want to visit the Great Wall of China. You may need one month to do this and £10,000. This could be the first money pot you begin saving towards.

When I did this exercise the first item on my list was a Cherry Blossom Tree. I don't know why, but I imagined myself walking around Japan in April surrounded by the blush-tinted blooms in Maruyama Park, Mount Yishino, Himeji Castle and Fuji Five Lakes. My second item was a mint green electric guitar as I imagined myself playing 'Streets of London,' a song my father used to play to me as a child - a time when I felt utter happiness and joy. When I'd completed my desires list, I walked upstairs to my bedroom and looked out of my window. There was a Cherry Blossom tree next door that had just started to bloom. I had never seen it before, and whether I just hadn't noticed it or whether I manifested it that day, it didn't matter. It was a sign that I was capable, willing and deserving to create. I was worthy. I mattered. Nature had shown me this.

You are worthy of desires. You are *safe* to desire.

CHAPTER 67
SAVING - START SMALL

S o many of you will read this headline and think ... but I don't have a lot of money to save! I don't have spare money. Let me bust this myth, too (whilst wagging my little finger like Nanny Mcphee). The fastest way to build wealth is to adjust your spending habits so that you can save more, be conscious about your spending and be proactive rather than reactive. It all starts with small amounts of money. Small, smart decisions with money, consistently and with the asset of time, create financial security for the rest of your life.

How much could you start saving today with the intention of leaving it untouched for your future self? How about redirecting the cost of a coffee into a savings account? There are some clever money apps around now that you can plug into your bank account for rounding up your purchases. These small round-ups could be money for using in a crisis or to cover Christmas gifts. Or how about a regular investment that could be set up with a monthly direct debit?

I have a future book in me to share my knowledge with you about investing (or if you want to get started now take a peek at our online investing course at www.catherinemorgan.com) but the message here is this: Compound your money habits by starting small. Take the emotion out of the equation and make it super easy for yourself. Our brains will struggle to understand time and uncertainty so do yourself a favour and just get started. Worry about the details later. It is less about how much and more about for how long.

CHAPTER 68
INFLATION AND RISK

We cannot move from Financial Growth to Financial Freedom without understanding risk and inflation. Many of us fear the word *risk* because what we are really saying is 'do I want to risk losing money?' and of course the answer is no! I can guarantee that most of you have some money in cash right now, or have had in the past. When we leave money in the bank, we are already taking a risk unless we spend that money - because of inflation. *Inflation* is the measure of the cost of living and the increase of cost of goods and services over time. Put simply, if the rate of inflation is 3% and you are earning less than that in cash, you are *losing* money. So if you had £100,000 in the bank earning 0.5% and inflation is at 3% your £100,000 would be worth £97,485 at the end of the year.

We need to reframe the word 'risk'! It is really about volatility and uncertainty and the level of uncertainty depends on whether it is needed for your fridge, larder or freezer. Your future self can accept more uncertainty because the future IS uncertain.

We need to keep some money in cash but only for our present self. You want money for now, money for soon and money for later.

How much money does my present self need? You need two amounts set aside:

- An amount for my Fridge (Financial Security) Pot £
- An amount for my Larder pots (1-5 years of planned expenditure) £

Fill in the amounts above. Here is a suggestion of where you could store it:

Pot #1: Find a high interest account for your financial security fund. This is money that you need in the next 12 months or if something happens. I suggest a minimum of six months living expenses (not income).

Pot #2: Find a 1-year fixed rate account - this is money that you need in one year.

Pot #3: Find a 2-year fixed rate account - this is money that you need in two years.

Pot #4: Find a 3-year fixed rate account - this is money that you need in three years.

Pot #5: Find a 4-year fixed rate account - this is money that you need in four years.

Pot #6: Find a 5-year fixed rate account - this is money that you need in five year's time

When it matures, roll it over for the same period if you don't use it, or use it to top up your financial security fund. A bigger security fund will provide more safety and security. Once this pot feels safe, which will be different for everyone (notice no *shoulding* here!) it will be time to think about filling up the freezer.

Call your bank and ask them to change the name of the pots to your selected name. Give every pound a purpose! Log the amounts on your financial closet organiser and track the growth each time you have a money date with yourself. Do this at the start of the year, too. Create an opening balance for yourself and a closing balance on 31st December.

CHAPTER 69
THE RULE OF 71
HOW LONG WOULD IT TAKE TO DOUBLE YOUR MONEY?

Take the rate of interest that you earn on your savings account and ask yourself how many years it would take to double your money. If you're earning 7% per year, that tells you that if you take 71 and divide it by 7 you get 10. Every 10 years, therefore, your money will double.

If you invest £5 per day into a children's pension from birth to the age of 10, with the current free tax relief from the government your child could have over £1 million invested by the time they retire. Some of you will think that £5 per day is a lot of money ... change this to 50p per day and they would have £100,000 by the time they are 65! This is based on a few assumptions of returns and inflation which are of course not guaranteed but isn't it awesome?!

You want growth year in year out ... you want the power of compound interest. This isn't money that you'll need to access in the near future. This is money for your future self. It requires different thinking.

CHAPTER 70

TOP 4 INVESTING MYTHS

Top 4 Investing Myths

The key thing to remember with saving, investing and speculating is that there is a massive difference between these three things. It all comes down to risk and time. Saving is putting money aside, most likely into the bank ... your fridge pot! The benefit of doing this is that you'll have access to that money fairly easily, and it will earn interest - a small bonus for depositing or lending that money to the bank. The bank will invest that money, but the interest for you will be a nominal amount. So if you put £100 in the bank, you don't want to risk that it's not going to be worth £100 when you need to access it. Holding money in cash is for short-term needs and wants.

Myth 1. *Investing is gambling*

Investing is putting money aside for growth and profit. The dictionary definition of investing is as follows: *putting money into schemes with the expectation of achieving a profit.* I don't like the use of the word 'schemes'. It implies that something isn't legitimate, or is risky. The word 'profit', however, is really important, because investing is really about putting money into a company that you believe is going to make a profit. This doesn't mean you have to be an expert or have to predict how companies are going to perform – that's what you use investment specialists for. Even if you're in what's called a *tracker based investment*, there will be some companies making a profit and some not, and that's the real risk of investing.

For this reason, investing in individual companies is perceived to be a higher risk. It makes sense: if you buy shares in *Apple* and the share price goes up, you make a profit. But if the share price goes down, you make a loss. In order to reduce the investing risk, think about building a basket of investments in more than one company. Hedge your bets – *Apple* shares go down but *John Lewis* (for example) shares go up. I invest in *Very Vanilla* investments, globally diversified with a range of asset classes like bonds, cash and shares. I like to invest ethically so that my investments are in line with my core values.

In order to be prepared for investing, consider what level of risk you should or should not be taking with your money. Another way to think of risk is to think of it as 'uncertainty'. The level of risk that you need to take is probably not even as much as you think. The risk you take and the return you get all relate to the amount of time you can invest for and what you're investing for. You would not invest money for things that you are going to spend on in the next few years. That would be risky!

So think about two things – time and purpose. What are you investing for? How long are you able to invest for? The general rule is that if you don't have at least five years to invest then you shouldn't be investing. Investing should be to fill up that Freezer pot. You will need sufficient time to ride out the uncertainties in the stock market.

The myth that investing is gambling is related to *speculating*, putting your money at risk and hoping that you'll get a higher return in a short period of time. You don't know if it will pay off, you're speculating. You might speculate on something like Bitcoin, for example. Speculating is a very different concept from investing, and it is important to remember that the two are not the same! Failing to understand the difference prevents us from investing in the first place - an even bigger risk because if you hold all your money in cash you are subject to inflation risk.

Myth 2. *Cash is investing*

Storing your cash in your fridge for daily access gives you the benefit of security and ease of access. You know that any money you hold in a UK FCA-regulated bank is protected up to a certain limit per person, per institution. In addition, the fridge is not locked and you can get in any time. Your cash may grow a little with interest, but the risk is that you'll be affected by inflation.

Take a Mars bar. In 2000 a Mars bar cost 29p. By 2020 it had gone up to 68p. Imagine how much harder your £1 has had to work in order to hedge against that increase.

Generally speaking, inflation is around 2% each year in the UK, so your £100 sitting in that bank account is reduced by £2 every year. Even with the top rate of interest in the UK right now (around 1.3%) your money is going up by 1.3% but down by 2%. If you're going to spend that money in the short term then that's fine. It won't stay there long enough to feel the impact of inflation.

As women, we tend to hold more cash than men. The statistics show that a considerably higher number of women than men hold cash ISAs. We have a fear of investing. A study by YouGov found that 55% of UK women said they had never held an investment, compared to 37% of men.

Myth 3. *Investing is only for the wealthy*

I'm passionate about helping women to manage their own money, and one of the big problems we have right now is that we don't know how to get started with investing. Getting financial advice can be costly for the average investor who has £100 per month to invest.

You don't actually need to seek financial advice to get started. As long as you have a basic level of knowledge and education you're perfectly capable of making these decisions for yourself. And you can get started with just £1.

Women are great at sticking to investment decisions. Once we've built that knowledge and got started, we're less likely to be influenced by human biases. Women are less likely to follow the herd. We're less likely to try to buy at the 'best' perceived time in comparison to men. It's not about timing *the* market, it's about timing *in* the market. It's not just about picking the right time to invest, it's about picking funds that match your time horizons and your purpose.

Think hard about the time you have and your purpose for saving or investing that money.

Myth 4. *You need a lump sum to get started*

For some investments this is true, but there are opportunities to invest without a lump sum. The best way to get started is with a regular monthly contribution.

In May 2019 I tested this by setting up a regular monthly contribution into a well-known stocks and shares ISA. Nine months later it's worth about £250, having grown by about 13%. And I'd kind of forgotten about it because I got so used to seeing it go out of my account and didn't miss that £25 every month. If I were to leave it to grow, over a period of time it could build up to a considerable amount of money. The purpose of that money is my children's university funds. In the same year I set up personal pensions for my children with a £30 per month contribution. Have you heard of these? If you invest just £1 per day from when they are born to age 20, assuming a 7% growth return and current government tax relief, by the age of 20 your children's pension could be worth £420,000 at age 65. That's right – just £1 per day!

Choose a small amount of money that you can afford to invest, and think about committing this money to your future self, your financial independence. Even in a happy relationship, every woman should have an investment in their own name. A stocks and shares ISA is a great way to do this.

The next step is to learn how to get started. Every month that you invest in the stock market, you're buying units. If you're in a fund – think of a fund like a basket of lots of different company shares – and investing every month, then every month you're buying a certain amount of units in that fund. If the markets go up, you're buying less for your money because the cost of each unit has gone up. When the markets are coming down, you're buying more for each £1. You can reduce your risk by, rather than committing one large amount of money at one time, drip feeding your investment monthly so that you average out the cost of buying into that fund. This is called pound cost averaging and is a great way to get started.

Ok - so I said I wasn't going to cover investing in this book but as you can see these myths stop us from even getting started!

CHAPTER 71

GROWING YOUR WEALTH

THE SIX MOST POWERFUL LESSONS I HAVE LEARNED

1. Step into trust, not control

Part of the state of receiving money more comfortably is to learn to surrender to what will be, to trust and accept that everything is OK and to let go of the need to try and control everything.

I bet many of you have money narratives like:

'I want to be in control of money'

'I want to have more control with money'

I have found myself using these expressions from time to time.

Having control over somebody or something is really a smoke screen for wanting to feel safe. We actually don't need to be in control at all! And we shouldn't confuse control with choices, or control with safety. We just want to feel safe, right?! In order to feel safe, we need to accept that there will be ebbs and flows of money in our life. Times when it comes in abundance and times when it does not.

The more we try to control something, the more out of control we become.

So how would it be if you stopped trying to control and just let go? Created more trust and space? Created space for the ebbs and flows?

What do I need to do to create space for money?

What control do I need to let go of?

What is the opposite of control?

What does that look like?

What do I need to do next to create this for myself?

What would be possible if I trusted myself more?

Looking back on my relationship with money, I wish I had known the following:

2. Get close but not obsessive about your spending

This is not to fill yourself with guilt or shame about your spending but to move closer to your habits and closer to the language you are using with money.

Invest time in learning how to create a simple method of managing money that works for you. If you are in a job, don't just think about your next pay rise. Consider the relationship you have with the money you earn. If you don't understand your spending habits it doesn't matter how much comes in - you will always spend more than you earn. Turn this around: *the more you earn, the more you should save.* Pay your future self as much as your current self. It starts with a little bit of money saved over time - small savings habits create big future savings.

Case Study: One Saturday afternoon I sat down with my two boys to play Monopoly. It is one of our favourite family games. (Plus, I always win!) What was super interesting to me was that my eldest son George had the most cash in his pile. He had five £500 notes and everyone else had only one or none at all. But it was his comment about the number of notes that I was so curious about.

He said: 'Mum, I feel broke'. I reminded him that he was the wealthiest out of all of us, but then I stopped ...

In my financial coaching training programme, I teach my students to be curious about people's language. He *felt* broke. Yet he had the largest amount of money.

I asked him: 'What would make you feel less broke?' He answered: 'I could count it, Mum...'

'What else?' I asked. 'I could exchange the £500 for £100 notes instead?'

'Sure. How would you feel if you were to do that?' 'Hmmm, probably the same, Mum.'

'How would you know if you were really broke?' 'I guess when I have £1 left!'

I felt proud that he came to that conclusion, but it was about how he felt. I could have just told him that this would make no difference to how much money he actually had but I held the space for him to come to the conclusion himself. I reflected his own words back so that he could hear them.

This is so powerful.

How often do we seek to solve rather than seek to listen? Next time you hear yourself or others sharing their feelings about money, hold the space for them and be curious about their beliefs. Reflect their language back to them and see what happens.

3. Respect time AND money

Give yourself TIME to improve your self-worth and self-belief. As you get older you'll care less about what others think anyway! If I had listened to this advice I wouldn't have tried so hard to fit into a jigsaw mould of who I thought I *should* be.

4. Focus on the things you can do and let go of the things you can't

Talk to someone - don't bury your head in the sand - a friend, sister, sometimes even a stranger. Accept that there are things in life you just can't control and that seeking control will only keep you stuck in feeling anxiety around money.

5. Pursue happiness, not wealth

Value experiences over things. *Instagram, Facebook, Snapchat, Pinterest* all encourage us to purchase and have 'stuff' in our lives. Don't be emotionally blackmailed about how perfect your life should be. Just live it. Show up every day and be proud of who you are.

Imagine being at the end of your life and evaluating the time you had here on earth. What would be your ideal legacy? Mine would be to have equipped one million women to be financially resilient, to have opportunities to make their own decisions irrelevant of their money, wealth and relationship. I would feel, then, that I've achieved my purpose, done the best I can and been the best version of myself.

6. Always look ahead as if we are already there

When we step into the future, as we mentioned earlier in this section, it creates uncertainty. Reframe this. Rather than looking ahead, look at the here and now and ask yourself: 'What life do I desire to be living right now?' Then step into it as if you are *already* living it.

What beliefs do you need to let go of to support living this life? State it in the present. 'I have let go of....(fill in the negative or limiting belief)'

What is *now* possible for you? 'I am now...' (add in the life you now have)

Set up a group on social media, or exchange an audio message with your best friend and share this every day. Hearing your own voice speaking this out loud is a very powerful act of manifestation, intention and desire.

If you are struggling with what life you desire, go back to the *desires* exercise or think about the things you want to be doing on a practical level.

Activity: *My Wealthy Woman Plan*

Here, you will identify the actions or small steps to take for yourself for the next week, month, three months, six months, 12 months and then future self beyond 12 months. This is useful because we find it hard to think too far into the future. If someone asked me where I want to be in five or 10 years I'd have no idea, but I do know where I want to be next week or next month, or maybe in a few months' time, or maybe even towards the end of the year. Beyond that, I find it difficult to focus. And many women I coach feel the same.

Go back to the closet exercise you did. What have you identified that needs resolving? Maybe you want to put something in that investing column and if now is not the right time to do it, perhaps by the end of the year you'll be in a position to start investing. You don't have to be specific now with deadlines and actions - this is just a very gentle exercise to get you feeling the intention.
When we focus on the detail too early, we get back into a scarcity mindset or survival mode. Focusing on the bigger picture brings clarity, intention and small step action. It's about focusing forward, not backwards.

Take a piece of paper and write one word that describes how you'd like to be feeling in the next seven days. Safe? Secure? Do you want to feel protected? Do you want to feel calm with money? Do you want to feel stable? Keep things simple.

In the middle of your page, write the commitments you're going to make. If you want to feel more in control, more secure and more confident, what are your actions? What steps are you going to take? What one thing could you turn around for the next seven days? Do you want to be a little bit more carefree? What do you want to use more of in the next week? What do you want to use less of? If you're high on planning, how could you implement some spontaneity into your life for the next seven days? Think about two or three things that you could do.

At the bottom of the page, write your next steps. Are you going to give more? Spend more? Save more? Invest more? Are you going to organize more? What two or three steps could you take in the next seven days to get that confidence, to be more excited, to feel more secure? Set up an emergency fund? Look at your banking? Sort out your pension? Enquire about making a will? What will make you feel more secure?

Your next priority is to schedule that action. Don't just tell yourself you're going to make a will and then leave it at that. Put it in your diary - not on to-do lists or sticky notes. Put it on your calendar right now and then find someone that can hold you accountable. Accountability is everything.

We know that financial planning can send us into overwhelm - pension, life insurance, will, savings and investments, spending plans - so pick one thing to focus on for the next 30 days. In order to choose, ask yourself if you want to stay stuck or make changes. I know this is tough but you have a choice in terms of what you do to deal with this situation. You can build financial resiliency muscles or you can stay at home and feel terrible.

Go back to the new money narratives you've created and use them for the next 30 days: *I am good with money. I am confident with money. I am making steps towards my financial goals. I am deserving of stepping into wealth.*

And then, most importantly, how will you celebrate once you've done it? How will you celebrate when you've learned how to invest? Completed your spending plan? How will you celebrate when you've sorted out and decoded your financial paperwork?

CHAPTER 72
INVESTING IN YOURSELF

A s women, we often plod along thinking that we can do it all ourselves.

Together is always better in my book, so think about creating your financial circle. This Money Circle® is a circle of people that you trust and can communicate openly with. There are five key financial relationships that every woman needs to have in their circle:

1. An accountant
2. A bookkeeper
3. A financial planner
4. A financial coach
5. A therapist

CHAPTER 73
LEAVING A LEGACY

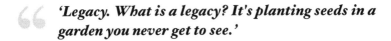

> *'Legacy. What is a legacy? It's planting seeds in a garden you never get to see.'*
>
> — **LIN-MANUEL MIRANDA**

I know many of you will not only want to create a wealthy life for yourself but also for others around you, your children, your children's children. Many of you will be thinking that leaving a legacy is about how much money you leave behind. I believe in the power of passing down *legacies of contribution* to the world, over solely passing down legacies of pots of money! Generational wealth is created by the passing-on of positive habits and behaviours with money as well as investments or assets.

I was hoping to avoid this word in this book, but an *asset* is just something that can be owned. If you are in debt, acquiring a debt asset and passing this onto future generations could be hugely problematic, so making sure that debts such as your mortgage are protected with life insurance is a must.

Acquire *meaningful* assets - stocks and shares portfolios, property, businesses, education, commodities like gold, wheat, coffee, platinum (my wedding ring has skyrocketed in value over the years). Once you have acquired meaningful assets, protect them. Speak to a financial professional about using trusts to protect this wealth. Make a will. I know, I know ... this means you have to address your mortality. But in reality, we are all going to outlive our bodies one day - best that it be in the way you want.

Make sure you have nominated beneficiaries for your meaningful assets. This means that it goes to who you want it to go to as quickly and easily as possible. Check your pension pots and ask your providers who you have nominated.

We'll go right back to the four stages of wealth creation:

1. Financial Insecurity
2. Financial Security
3. Financial Growth
4. Financial Freedom

The blocks to reaching financial freedom are the unforeseen: illness, accidents or - worst case scenario - the end of our lives. This is where I get my Nanny McFee finger out again and wag it at you ... *Please* pay this some attention. It will be the best thing you ever did.

Once your life is protected you can focus on living a life of financial freedom, in which you can achieve your full potential and self-actualisation. For me, part of this is about leaving the ego behind, the exterior display of wealth that brings very little long-term fulfilment - the flash cars, the unnecessary purchases. Financial freedom is about creating a legacy for those you love, about feeling safe to give money for the purpose of what this freedom creates for ourselves and others. *Freedom* in itself is about not feeling restricted or confined ... a state of freeness.

It is important to define financial freedom for yourself. For some it is paying off their mortgage. For others it is being able to give back philanthropically. It may be more about being financially independent.

What is financial freedom for you?

How would you know when you are living in it?

What is important to you about that?

Self-actualisation, as Maslow described it, is about how you can use money to achieve personal growth and fulfilment. It is not about how others see you and treat you, but how you treat yourself. How can we use the money we have accumulated to feel loved? Be loved? Give love?

I imagine myself with an abundance of wealth that I can use for causes that I feel are based on injustice in the world - women stuck in abusive, narcissistic relationships suffering from financial abuse, or victims of sexual abuse who don't get the right support when they need it.

Saving money for your future self is key for how to create generational wealth and financial freedom.

CHAPTER 74
END - 3 STEPS TO BECOME A WEALTHY WOMAN

This is not really the end. An 'end' insinuates a point when being a wealthy woman ceases to exist. I don't want you to come to the end of this book and sit in fear or guilt or shame. I want you to know that all of this is all possible for you. Right now. Today.

Today is the day that you can decide to take action: to nurture your relationship with money, to empower yourself, to heal and look forward to a financial future that is filled with love, gratitude and self-empowerment. You can change the narrative you use with yourself and in so doing you will change the blueprint of your family. Today is the day you not only change the relationship you have with yourself and *your* financial future, but for every future generation - your daughters, your sons, your grandchildren. Every single future generation.

You are safe to take this next step.

You are safe to deserve more wealth, create more wealth and grow more wealth.

It is safe for me to take responsibility with money.

It is safe for me to enjoy today and look to the future.

It is safe for me to save and spend.

It is safe for me to spend money on myself with no guilt.

It is safe for me to be impulsive and feel secure.

It is not *just* about the money. *Deserve* more, *create* more, *grow* more. Here's to celebrating you as you Step into Wealth® to become that wealthy woman you already are.

Catherine x

ABOUT THE AUTHOR

Catherine Morgan is a multi-award winning qualified Financial Planner and award-winning Certified Financial Coach, on a mission to reduce financial anxiety and increase financial empowerment & resilience for 1 billion women around the world.

Featured as one of the top 32 female entrepreneurs to look out for in *Business Leader,* she is host of the top 1% global podcast *In Her Financial Shoes,* founder of *The Money Panel*®, winner of the Money Marketing 'Financial Wellbeing Champion' of the year 2021, Marketing Influencer of the year for *Professional Adviser 2021,* highly commended for 'Role Model of the Year 2019' in *Women in Financial Services and* winner of Best New Business in the National Business Women's Awards 2019.

facebook.com/catherine.morgan.92560
linkedin.com/in/catherine-morgan
instagram.com/catherinemorganmoney
youtube.com/catherinemorganmoney

RESOURCES

To complete the Money StoryTypes™ *Quiz, head over to www. itsnotaboutthemoney.com/quiz*

To find all the resources mentioned in this book, head over to www. itsnotaboutthemoney.com/tools

ENDNOTES

12. TRAUMA AND THE 4 TRAUMA RESPONSES

1. Complex PTSD: From Surviving to Thriving: A GUIDE AND MAP FOR RECOVERING FROM CHILDHOOD TRAUMA, 2013
2. https://www.starlingbank.com/campaign/makemoneyequal/

13. ENERGY

1. *Rapid Transformational Therapy* - Marissa Peer

15. HABITS AND BEHAVIOURS

1. *In the realm of hungry ghosts*, Gabor Mate, Vintage Canada, 2009
2. Carl Jung, 1875-1961
3. Nikki Myers *Yoga of 12-Step Recovery https://www.offthematintotheworld.org/nikki-myers*

20. OVERWORKING AND UNDEREARNING

1. Eye Movement Desensitization and Reprocessing (EMDR)
2. Matrix Reimprinting https://www.matrixreimprinting.com/what-is-matrix.asp

23. CARRIED EMOTIONS

1. Gemma Cairney Instagram account (@gemcairn)

25. YOUR FINANCIAL BLUEPRINT

1. *The Biology of Belief,* Dr Bruce Lipton, Hay House UK, 2011
2. *Atomic Habits*, James Clear, Avery Publishing Group, 2018

30. DESIRES AND DERAILERS

1. Sociologist, Dr. Morris Massey http://changingminds.org/explanations/values/values_development.htm

SMALL STEP #2

1. Starling Bank www.starlingbank.com

34. WHAT IS STOPPING YOU FROM BEING IN FLOW?

1. Milahy Csikszentmihalyi *'The Psychology of Optimal Experience'* Harper Perennial Modern Classics (10 July 2008)
2. Sawyer (2015) and Kotler (2014) www.stevenkotler.com

42. 3 WAYS TO TACKLE MONEY ALREADY SPENT (DEBT)

1. Dave Ramsey - debt snowballing method www.ramseysolutions.com

46. THE STRONG MODEL TO BUILD FINANCIAL TRUST

1. University College London (UCL) www.ucl.ac.uk

53. FINANCIAL REGRETS

1. Hargreaves Lansdown, www.hl.co.uk
2. *The Top Five Regrets of the Dying*, Bronnie Ware, Hay House UK, 2012.

54. LAW OF SUBTRACTION

1. *The Laws of Subtraction: 6 Simple Rules for Winning in the Age of Excess Everything*, Matthew E. May, McGraw Hill Education, 2012

58. THE MONTHLY MONEY DATE

1. International Journal of Yoga, 2011 https://www.ijoy.org.in

Printed in Great Britain
by Amazon